Official Documents of the Little Big Horn

The Little Big Horn 1876

The Official Communications, Documents and Reports

With Rosters of the Officers and Troops of the Campaign

Compiled and annotated by

Loyd J. Overfield II

University of Nebraska Press
Lincoln and London

Copyright © 1971 by the Arthur H. Clark Company
Manufactured in the United States of America

First Bison Book printing: 1990
Most recent printing indicated by the last digit below:
10   9   8   7   6   5   4   3   2   1

Library of Congress Cataloging-in-Publication Data
Overfield, Loyd J.
The Little Big Horn, 1876: the official communications,
documents, and reports, with rosters of the officers and troops of
the campaign / compiled and annotated by Loyd J. Overfield.
p. cm.
Reprint. Originally printed: Glendale, Calif. : A. H. Clark, 1971.
ISBN 0-8032-8601-5
1. Little Big Horn, Battle of the, 1876. 2. United States. Army.
Cavalry, 7th—Registers. 3. Cheyenne Indians—Wars, 1876—Sources.
4. Dakota Indians—Wars, 1876—Sources. I. Title.
E83.876.09   1990
973.8'2—dc20   90-12353
CIP

Reprinted by arrangement with the Arthur H. Clark Company

A foldout showing portraits of the twelve Seventh Cavalry officers who
died with Custer has been omitted from this Bison Book edition.

Contents

Illustrations

Acknowledgments

I would like very much to acknowledge the help I received in many forms from the following:

The late R. B. MacLaine Sr., Tacoma, Washington
The Little Big Horn Associates
The National Archives, Old Military Records
    Section
The Library, Bell Hall, Fort Leavenworth
The Leavenworth, Kansas, Public Library and Staff
The Oceanside, California, Public Library and Staff
The Carlsbad, California, Public Library and Staff
Lisle G. Brown, Salt Lake City, Utah

To my wife, Toni, for patience

and especially to George Kealy, without whom I would never have written this.

Preface

On June 25th, 1876, Lieutenant Colonel George Armstrong Custer, at the head of five companies of the 7th United States Cavalry rode into battle against the hostile Sioux and Northern Cheyenne Indians encamped on the Little Big Horn River. By the time night fell, Custer, a Brevet Major-General for Civil War service, and all of the two-hundred-odd officers and men with him were dead.

In the more than ninety-four years since that June day in 1876, "Custer's Last Stand," as that fight is now popularly known, has become a subject of seemingly never-ending controversy. A legion of students and historians, both amateur and professional; writing a host of books, have examined practically every aspect of this engagement in the minutest detail. The variety of explanations or condemnations arrived at for any particular action or lack of action is truly astounding.

Having read most of the volumes published about General Custer, I have noticed that more frequently than not, when official documents are quoted it is done in extracts and often garbled and out of context. It is my desire to provide here a compilation of many of the official letters, orders, reports, telegrams etc. which pertain to the Battle of the Little Big Horn, quoted in their entirety directly from microfilms of the original documents supplied to me by the National Archives (except Document 4 as noted). A brief explanation of each document is added in footnote form.

The documents reproduced are limited to those dated within the year 1876. An additional document of importance is one dated January 27, 1877, being the report of Lieutenant George D. Wallace on the march of the Seventh Cavalry from June 22 to 25, 1876. This report is to be found as an appendix to the extensive journal and narrative of Lieutenant Edward J. McClernand in the second volume of the present series.

As appendices, I have prepared a chronological list of the engagements with the hostiles that summer; a series of Tables of Organization for the various bodies of troops who were campaigning in the field; and in addition I have prepared copies of the Muster Rolls for each of the companies which was in the vicinity of the Little Big Horn, taken again directly from microfilms of the original rolls.

Collected over a period of several years, the copies of these documents and rolls have provided me with many hours of enjoyment and given me answers to many of the questions I had about the Battle of the Little Big Horn, the men who fought there and the ones who didn't. I sincerely hope that you will find them as enjoyable and informative.

Garryowen!   L. J. OVERFIELD II

The Transmittal of Custer's Request for Duty, and Terry's Endorsement

The Communications, Documents and Reports

1

Saint Paul, Minn.   May sixth (6) [1876]
Adjutant General, Division Missouri, Chicago

I forward the following to his excellency, the President, through military channels:

I have seen your order transmitted thro' the General of the Army, directing that I be not permitted to accompany the expedition about to move against hostile Indians. As my entire regiment forms a part of the proposed expedition and as I am the senior officer of the regiment on duty in this department, I respectfully but most earnestly request that while not allowed to go in command of the expedition, I may be permitted to serve with my regiment in the field. I appeal to you as a soldier to spare me the humiliation of seeing my regiment march to meet the enemy and I to not share its dangers.

(signed) G. A. CUSTER
Brevet Maj. Gen. U.S.A.

In forwarding the above I wish to say expressly that I have no desire whatever to question the orders of the President, or of any of my military superiors, whether Lieutenant Colonel Custer shall be permitted to accompany my column or not, I shall go in command of it. I do not know the reasons upon which the orders

NOTE: Colonel Custer was ordered by President Grant to remain at Fort Abraham Lincoln while the 7th Cavalry marched on the summer's campaigns under Major M. A. Reno. General Terry, at Custer's request, interceded on Custer's behalf.

already given rest, but if those reasons do not forbid it, Lieutenant Colonel Custer's services would be very valuable with his regiment.

(signed) TERRY
Commanding Department

Official copy respectfully furnished by mail.

R. C. DRUM
Assistant Adjutant General

2

(copy)
Telegram

HEADQUARTERS MILITARY DIVISION OF THE MISSOURI

Chicago, Illinois, May 7th 1876

Brigadier General E. D. Townsend,
Washington, D.C.

The following dispatch from General Terry is respectfully forwarded. I am sorry Lieutenant Colonel Custer did not manifest as much interest by staying at his post to organize and get ready his regiment and the expedition as he does now to accompany it. On a previous occasion in eighteen sixty-eight (1868) I asked executive clemency for Colonel Custer to enable him to accompany his regiment against the Indians, and I sincerely hope if granted this time it will have sufficient effect to prevent him from again attempting to throw discredit on his profession and his brother officers.

(signed) P. H. Sheridan
Lieut. General

NOTE: This endorsement by General Sheridan refers to the time in 1868, when Sheridan was instrumental in getting Custer restored to duty from a sentence of suspension and loss of pay imposed by a Court Martial.

3

copy
telegram

Washington, D.C., May 8, 1876

General A. H. Terry
St. Paul, Minn.

The dispatch of General Sheridan enclosing yours of yesterday touching General Custer's urgent request to go under your command with his regiment, has been submitted to the President who sends me word that if you want General Custer along he withdraws his objections. Advise Custer to be prudent not to take along any newspaper men who always work mischief, and to abstain from any personalities in the future. Tell him I want him to confine his whole mind to his legitimate office, and trust to time. That newspaper paragraph in the New York World of May 2nd., compromised his best friends here, and almost deprived us of the ability to serve him.

(signed) W. T. SHERMAN
General

NOTE: Permission to accompany his regiment was finally granted by the President, and General Sherman sent these words of warning to Custer.

4

HEADQUARTERS DEPARTMENT OF DAKOTA

In the Field Camp
near Fort Abraham Lincoln, D.T.
May 14, 1876

GENERAL FIELD-ORDERS
No. 1.

The Department Commander hereby assumes, in person, the command of the force organized for field operations.

The following named officers will act upon the staff:

Captain E. W. Smith, 18th Infantry, Acting Assistant Adjutant General.

Assistant Surgeon J. W. Williams, Chief Medical Officer.

Captain O. E. Michaelis, Ordance Officer

1st Lieutenant H. J. Nowland, 7th Cavalry, Quartermaster

1st Lieutenant Edward Maguire, Corps of Engineers

Lieutenant Nowlan [*sic*] will discharge his duties upon the staff of the Department Commander in addition to those of Regimental Quartermaster.

The Indian Scouts will report to Lieutenant Colonel Custer, 7th Cavalry, for duty with his regiment. All interpreters, guides and other civil employees in the pay

NOTE: As stated in the May 6th communication (Document 1), General Terry personally commanded the expedition. This is the order designating his field staff. From *United States Army and Navy Journal,* July 1, 1876, vol. XIII, no. 47, p. 754.

of the Quartermaster's Department will report to Lieutenant H. J. Nowlan, Quartermaster of the force in the field, to be by him assigned to duty under direction of the Department Commander.

By Command of Brigadier General Terry

Ed. W. Smith, 18th Infantry,
Acting Assistant Adjutant General

5

HEADQUARTERS DEPARTMENT OF DAKOTA
(In the Field)

Camp on Powder River, June 10, 1876.

SPECIAL FIELD ORDERS
NO. 11.

1. The Quartermaster of the expedition is hereby ordered to purchase, for public use, two Mackinac boats, at a price not to exceed twenty-five dollars apiece.

2. Major M. A. Reno, 7th Cavalry, with six companies (the right wing) of his regiment, and one gun from the Gatling battery, will proceed, at the earliest practicable moment, to make a reconnoissance of the Powder River from the present camp to the mouth of the Little Powder. From the last-named point he will cross to the head waters of Mizpah Creek, and descend that creek to its junction with Powder River; thence he will cross the Pumpkin Creek and Tongue River, and descend the Tongue to its junction with the Yellowstone – where he may expect to meet the remaining companies of the 7th Cavalry and supplies of subsistence and forage.

NOTE: The expedition left Fort Abraham Lincoln on May 17, 1876. On June 10th General Terry issued these orders to Major Reno for a scout with Companies B, C, E, F, I, and L, 7th Cavalry. Reno left camp about 3 p.m. on the 10th. During the course of this scout, on June 17th, Reno was within forty miles of the scene of General Crook's Battle of the Rosebud. This command reached Colonel John Gibbon's camp on June 18th. The eight scouts were four Dakota: Bear Waiting, Buffalo Ancestor, Caroo, and White Cloud; and three or four Arikara: Forked Tongue, One Feather, Young Hawk, and possibly Tall Bear who was rejected because his horse gave out.

Major Reno's command will be supplied with subsistence for twelve days, and with forage for the same period, at the rate of two pounds of grain per day for each animal.

The guide, Mitch Bouyer, and eight Indian Scouts, to be detailed by Lieutenant Colonel Custer, will report to Major Reno for duty with his column.

Acting Assistant Surgeon J. E. Porter * is detailed for duty with Major Reno.

By Command of Brigadier General Terry:

ED. W. SMITH,
Captain 18th Infantry, A.D.C.,
Acting Assistant Adjutant General

---

* The correct name of the Acting Assistant Surgeon was Henry R. Porter. The appearance here of the initials "J. E." was, no doubt, a mistake of Captain Smith or of a clerk who copied the order. James E. Porter was an officer of Captain Keogh's Company i, and was killed on June 25th.

6

In the Field, Camp at mouth of Tongue River

June 20, 1876

SPECIAL FIELD ORDERS

NO. 15

Lieutenant-Colonel Custer, Commanding 7th Cavalry, will proceed without unnecessary delay, with the Headquarters and six companies of his regiment, the Indian Scouts, and the Gatling battery now at this camp, to the point occupied by the camp of Major Reno's command, where he will assume command of the force there assembled, and to-morrow proceed with it to the mouth of Rosebud River, where he will await for further orders.

By command of Brigadier General Terry.

(signed) ED. W. SMITH

Captain, 18th Infantry, A.D.C.

Acting Assistant Adjutant General

NOTE: Learning that Major Reno had reached Colonel Gibbon's camp, General Terry issued orders for Custer to join him. From microfilm copy, National Archives, File #6160, Adjutant General's Office, 1876.

7

HEADQUARTERS DEPARTMENT OF DAKOTA
(In the Field)

Camp at Mouth of Rosebud River,
Montana, June 22nd, 1876.

Lieut. Col. G. A. Custer, 7th Cavalry.

Colonel:

The Brigadier-General Commanding directs that, as soon as your regiment can be made ready for the march, you will proceed up the Rosebud in pursuit of the Indians whose trail was discovered by Major Reno a few days since. It is, of course, impossible to give you any definite instructions in regard to this movement, and were it not impossible to do so, the Department Commander places too much confidence in your zeal, energy, and ability to wish to impose upon you precise orders which might hamper your action when nearly in contact with the enemy. He will however, indicate to you his own views of what your action should be, and he desires that you should conform to them unless you shall see sufficient reason for departing from them. He thinks that you should proceed up the Rosebud until you ascertain definitely the direction in which the trail above spoken of leads. Should it be found (as it appears almost certain that it will be found) to turn towards the Little Horn, he thinks that you should still proceed southward, perhaps as far as the headwaters of the Tongue, and then turn towards the Little Horn, feeling

NOTE: Having a fairly good idea (from Major Reno's report and from the reports of several scouts made by the 2nd Cavalry with Colonel Gibbon) that the Indians would be found in the vicinity of the Little Big Horn valley, these orders were given to Custer.

constantly, however, to your left, so as to preclude the possibility of the escape of the Indians to the south or southeast by passing around your left flank.

The column of Colonel Gibbon is now in motion for the mouth of the Big Horn. As soon as it reaches that point it will cross the Yellowstone and move up at least as far as the forks of the Big and Little Horns. Of course its further movements must be controlled by circumstances as they arise, but it is hoped that the Indians, if upon the Little Horn, may be so nearly inclosed by the two columns that their escape will be impossible. The Department Commander desires that on your way up the Rosebud you should thoroughly examine the upper part of Tullock's Creek, and that you should endeavor to send a scout through to Colonel Gibbon's Column, with information of the results of your examination. The lower part of the creek will be examined by a detachment from Colonel Gibbon's command.

The supply steamer will be pushed up the Big Horn as far as the forks if the river is found to be navigable for that distance, and the Department Commander, who will accompany the Column of Colonel Gibbon, desires you to report to him there not later than the expiration of the time for which your troops are rationed, unless in the meantime you receive further orders.

> Very Respectfully,
> Your Obedient Servant,
> ED. W. SMITH, Captain, 18th Infantry
> Acting Assistant Adjutant General

8

Camp on Little Big Horn,
20 miles from its mouth.
June 27".

General Terry:

I have had a most terrific engagement with the hostile Indians. They left their camp last evening at sundown moving due south in the direction of Big Horn Mountains. I am very much crippled and cannot possibly pursue. Lieutenants McIntosh and Hodgson and Dr. DeWolf are among the killed. I have many wounded and many horses and mules shot. I have lost both my own horses. I have not seen or heard from Custer since he ordered me to charge with my battalion (3 companies) promising to support me.

I charged about 2 P.M., but meeting no support was forced back to the hills. At this point I was joined by Benteen with 3 companies and the pack train rear guard (one Co.). I have fought thousands and can still hold my own, but cannot leave here on account of the wounded. Send me medical aid at once and rations.

M. A. RENO,
Maj. 7th Cavalry.

As near as I can say now I have over 100 men killed and wounded.

NOTE: Leaving General Terry's camp on June 23rd, the 7th Cavalry marched toward the Little Big Horn. On the 25th the Indian village was located and orders given for the attack. This message, entered as Exhibit #5 at Major Reno's Court of Inquiry, was delivered to General Terry as his column marched up the valley of the Little Big Horn on the morning of the 27th. The messages which Indian Scouts were unable to deliver during the night of the 26th may have been identical to this one.

9

(Telegram)

HEADQUARTERS DEPARTMENT OF DAKOTA,
Camp on Little Big Horn River, Montana,
June 27, 1876.

To the Adjutant General of
the Military Division of the Missouri,
Chicago, Ill., via Fort Ellis:

It is my painful duty to report that day before yesterday, the 25th instant, a great disaster overtook General Custer and the troops under his command. At 12 o'clock of the 22d he started with his whole regiment and a strong detachment of scouts and guides from the mouth of the Rosebud. Proceeding up that river about twenty miles, he struck a very heavy Indian trail which had previously been discovered, and, pursuing it, found that it led, as it was supposed it would lead, to the Little Big Horn River. Here he found a village of almost unexampled extent, and at once attacked it with that portion of his force which was immediately at hand. Major Reno, with three companies, A, G, and M, of the regiment, was sent into the valley of the stream, at the point where the trail struck it. General Custer, with five companies, C, E, F, I, and L, attempted to enter it about 3 miles lower down. Reno forded the river, charged down its left bank, dismounted, and fought on foot untill finally, completely overwhelmed by numbers, he was compelled to mount, recross the river, and seek a refuge

NOTE: The above, and the following document (10), are General Terry's first reports of the battle, carried to Fort Ellis, Montana, by the civilian scout, "Muggins" Taylor. Taylor left the command on July 1st and reached Fort Ellis the evening of the 3rd.

on the high bluffs which overlook its right bank. Just as he recrossed, Captain Benteen, who, with three companies, D, H, and K, was some two miles to the left of Reno when the action commenced, but who had been ordered by General Custer to return, came to the river, and, rightly concluding that it was useless for his force to attempt to renew the fight in the valley, he joined Reno on the bluffs. Captain McDougall, with his company, B, was at first some distance in the rear, with the train of pack-mules; he also came up to Reno. Soon this united force was nearly surrounded by Indians, many of whom, armed with rifles of long range, occupied positions which commanded the ground held by the cavalry – ground from which there was no escape. Rifle-pits were dug, and the fight was maintained, though with heavy loss, from about half past two o'clock of the 25th till 6 o'clock of the 26th, when the Indians withdrew from the valley, taking with them their village. Of the movements of General Custer and the five companies under his immediate command scarcely anything is known from those who witnessed them, for no officer or soldier who accompanied him has yet been found alive. His trail, from the point where Reno crossed the stream, passes along and in the rear of the crest of the bluffs on the right bank for nearly or quite three miles. Then it comes down to the bank of the river, but at once diverges from it as if he had unsuccessfully attempted to cross; then turns upon itself, almost completes a circle, and ceases. It is marked by the remains of his officers and men and the bodies of his horses, some of them dotted along the path, others heaped in ravines and upon knolls, where halts appear to have been made. There is abundant evidence that a gallant resistance was offered by the troops, but that they were beset on all sides by overpowering numbers. The officers known to be killed are: General Custer, Captains Keogh, Yates, and Custer, Lieutenants Cook, Smith, McIntosh, Calhoun, Porter, Hodgson, Sturgis, and Riley, of the cavalry; Lieutenant Crittenden, of the Twentieth Infantry; and Acting Assistant Surgeon DeWolf, Lieutenant Harrington, of the cavalry, and Assistant Surgeon Lord are missing; Captain Benteen and Lieutenant Varnum, of the cavalry are slightly wounded. Mr. Boston Custer, a brother, and Mr. Reed, a nephew, of General Custer, were with him and were killed. No other officers than those whom I have named are among the killed, wounded, and missing.

It is impossible as yet to obtain a nominal list of the enlisted men who were killed and wounded; but the number of killed, including officers, must reach 250; the number of wounded is 51. At the mouth of the Rosebud, I informed General Custer that I would take the supply-steamer Far West up the Yellowstone to ferry General Gibbon's column over the river; that I should personally accompany that column; and that it would, in all probability, reach the mouth of the Little Big Horn on the 26th instant. The steamer reached General Gibbon's troops, near the mouth of the Big Horn, early in the morning of the 24th, and at 4 o'clock in the afternoon all his men and animals were across the Yellowstone. At 5 o'clock, the column, consisting of five companies of the Seventh Infantry, four companies of the Second Cavalry, and a battery of three Gatling guns, marched out to and across Tullock's Creek. Starting soon after 5 o'clock in the morning of the 25th, the infantry made a march of twenty-two miles over the most difficult country I have ever seen. In order that scouts might be sent into the valley of the Little Big

Horn, the cavalry, with the battery, was then pushed on
thirteen or fourteen miles further, reaching camp at
midnight. The scouts were sent out at half past 4 in the
morning of the 26th. They soon discovered three Indians, who were at first supposed to be Sioux but, when
overtaken, they proved to be Crows, who had been with
General Custer. They brought the first intelligence of
the battle. Their story was not credited. It was supposed
that some fighting, perhaps severe fighting, had taken
place; but it was not believed that disaster could have
overtaken so large a force as twelve companies of cavalry. The infantry, which had broken camp very early,
soon came up, and the whole column entered and moved
up the valley of the Little Big Horn. During the afternoon efforts were made to send scouts through to what
was supposed to be General Custer's position, to obtain
information of the condition of affairs; but those who
were sent out were driven back by parties of Indians,
who, in increasing numbers, were seen hovering in General Gibbon's front. At twenty minutes before 9 o'clock
in the evening, the infantry had marched between
twentynine and thirty miles. The men were very weary
and daylight was fading. The column was therefore
halted for the night, at a point about eleven miles in a
straight line above the mouth of the stream. This morning the movement was resumed, and after a march of
nine miles, Major Reno's intrenched position was
reached. The withdrawal of the Indians from around
Reno's command and from the valley was undoubtedly
caused by the approach of General Gibbon's troops.
Major Reno and Captain Benteen, both of whom are
officers of great experience, accustomed to see large
masses of mounted men, estimate the number of Indians engaged at not less than twenty-five hundred.

Other officers think that the number was greater than this. The village in the valley was about three miles in length and about a mile in width. Besides the lodges proper, a great number of temporary brush-wood shelters was found in it, indicating that many men besides its proper inhabitants had gathered together there. Major Reno is very confident that there were a number of white men fighting with the Indians. I have as yet received no official reports in regard to the battle; but what is stated herein is gathered from the officers who were on the ground then and from those who have been over it since.

ALFRED H. TERRY
Brigadier General

10

(Telegram)

HEADQUARTERS DEPARTMENT OF DAKOTA
Camp on Little Horn, June 28, 1876

Assistant Adjutant General
Military Division of the Missouri, Chicago, Ill.:

The wounded were brought down from the bluffs last night and made as comfortable as our means would permit. To-day horse and hand litters have been constructed, and this evening we shall commence moving the wounded toward the mouth of the Little Big Horn, to which point I hope that the steamer has been able to come. The removal will occupy three or four days, as the marches must be short. A reconnaissance was made to-day by Captain Ball, of the Second Cavalry, along the trail made by the Indians when they left the valley. He reports that they divided into two parties, one of which kept the valley of Long Fork, making, he thinks, for the Big Horn Mountains; the other turned more to the eastward. He also discovered a very heavy trail leading into the valley that is not more than five days old. This trail is entirely distinct from the one which Custer followed, and would seem to show that at least two large bands united here just before the battle. The dead were all buried to-day.

ALFRED H. TERRY,
Brigadier General.

11

Camp on Little Big Horn
June 28th., 1876

Dear Major,

We will start down the river today for the steamboat with the wounded of Custer's command and from the mouth of this stream move down to the mouth of the Big Horn. Gen. Custer's command met with terrible disaster here on the 25th. Custer with 5 Co.'s were so far as we can ascertain, completely annihilated, no living man of them having yet been found and probably none of them escaped except two of our Crow scouts who were lent Custer by me and brought us the first news. Mitch Bouyer was killed, and the bodies of Gen. Custer, Col. C. (his brother) and another brother (citizen), Capts. Keogh and Yates, and Lieuts. Cooke, Adjt. Calhoun, *Porter, Riley, Sturgis* (son of the Gen.), Crittenden (2nd Inf., son of the Gen.), Hodgson, McIntosh, Harrington, Actg. Asst. Surgs. DeWolf and *Lord* have all been identified positively except those *underscored* [in italics].

On the 26th *we* made a long march till dark, came in sight of some few scattering Indians, and the next day (yesterday) reached Col. Reno's command fortified on the hill. They were in a desperate strait until 6 o'clock the night before (26th) with very little water and 50 wounded men and the Indians decamped in very great

NOTE: This letter from Colonel John Gibbon was to Captain D. W. Benham, Brevet Major, of the 7th Infantry, the commanding officer of Fort Ellis. This letter was also carried by the scout, "Muggins" Taylor. From Montana Historical Society, Contributions, vol. 4 (1903) pp. 284-86.

haste at our approach, leaving an immense quantity of plunder behind which we shall destroy today.

The delight of the poor fellows when they finally discovered us to be friends was extreme. Roughly stated, the loss of Custer's command is about one half, say 250 men. The Indians were in great strength and were estimated at from 1800 to 2500 *warriors*. My command is intact and in fine order, and I wish you would telegraph the C.O.'s Fort Shaw and Camp Baker that we are all well, to allay the anxiety of friends. I wish I knew where Mrs. Gibbon was that you might telegraph her but I do not. At a venture you might telegraph Mr. Henry Moale, 18 Commerce St., Baltimore, "Tell Fannie myself and command are all well. J.G." Date it "Camp on Little Big Horn, June 28th."

When the fight commenced Col. Reno with 3 Co.'s charged, had a heavy fight, was overpowered and driven back and took to the bluff's where he met 4 other Co's and they had heavy fighting all the rest of that day and all of the 26th knew nothing of the fate of Custer and his 5 co's until we arrived and informed them of it. 3 P.M. We have buried all the dead and I hope to have litters for the wounded finished in time to go a few miles down the river today, camp near the site of the Indian camp and destroy the property deserted by them. When you read this send it to Gen. A. J. Smith, Helena, who will please give it to Col. Broadwater at request of Carroll who is with us here.

Yours Truly.,
J. G.

Maj. Benham
Ft. Ellis.

12

(Telegram)

HEADQUARTERS DEPARTMENT OF DAKOTA
Camp on Yellowstone,
near Big Horn River, Montana,
July 2, 1876.

Lieut. Gen. P. H. Sheridan, Chicago, Ill.,
The Adjutant General, Military Division
   of the Missouri, Chicago, Ill.

In the evening of the 28th we commenced moving down the wounded, but were able to get on but four miles, as our hand-litters did not answer the purpose. The mule-litters did exceedingly well, but they were insufficient in number. The 29th, therefore, was spent in making a full supply of them. In the evening of the 29th we started again, and at 2 A.M. of the 30th the wounded were placed on a steamer at the mouth of the Little Big Horn. The afternoon of the 30th they were brought to the depot on the Yellowstone. I now send them by steamer to Fort Lincoln, and with them one of my aids, Capt. E. W. Smith, who will be able to answer any questions which you may desire to ask. I have

NOTE: This and the following telegram (Document 13), both dated July 2 and both to General Sheridan, were carried to Fort Lincoln by Captain E. W. Smith, General Terry's Adjutant, aboard the steamer "Far West," arriving on the 5th of July. The dispatches were telegraphed out the morning of the 6th, and Captain Smith then proceeded to report in person to General Sheridan. Due to a break in the line from Bozeman, Montana, Sheridan received these two letters before he received the reports carried by Taylor (see Documents 9 and 10). When the "confidential" dispatch was forwarded to the War Department in Washington, it was intercepted by a newsman and published in an evening newspaper of July 6th.

34

brought down the troops to this point. They arrived to-night. They need refitting, particularly in the matter of transportation, before starting again. Although I had on the steamer a good supply of subsistence and forage, there are other things which we need, and I should hesitate to trust the boat again in the Big Horn.

Colonel Sheridan's dispatch informing me of the reported gathering of Indians on the Rosebud, reached me after I came down here. I hear nothing of General Crook's movements.

At least a hundred horses are needed to mount the cavalrymen now here.

ALFRED H. TERRY,
Brigadier General.

13

(Telegram)
CONFIDENTIAL [to Gen. Sheridan]
HEADQUARTERS DEPARTMENT OF DAKOTA
Camp on Yellowstone,
near Big Horn River, Montana,
July 2, 1876

I think I owe it to myself to put you more fully in possession of the facts of the late operations. While at the mouth of the Rosebud I submitted my plan to Genl. Gibbon and General Custer. They approved it heartily. It was that Custer with his whole regiment should move up the Rosebud till he should meet a trail which Reno had discovered a few days before but that he should send scouts over it and keep his main force further to the south so as to prevent the Indians from slipping in between himself and the mountains. He was also to examine the headwaters of Tullock's creek as he passed it and send me word of what he found there. A scout was furnished him for the purpose of crossing the country to me. We calculated it would take Gibbon's column until the twenty-sixth to reach the mouth of the Little Big Horn and that the wide sweep which I had proposed Custer should make would require so much time that Gibbon would be able to cooperate with him in attacking any Indians that might be found on that stream. I asked Custer how long his marches would be. He said they would be about at first about thirty miles a day. Measurements were made and calculation based on that rate of progress. I talked with him about his strength and at one time suggested that perhaps it would be well for me to take Gibbon's cavalry and go with him. To this suggestion he replied that without reference to the command he would prefer his own regiment alone. As a homogeneous body, as much could be done with it as with the two combined and he expressed the utmost confidence that he had all the force that he could need, and I shared his confidence. The plan adopted was the only one that promised to bring the Infantry into action and I desired to make sure of things by getting up every available man. I offered Custer the battery of Gatling guns but he declined it saying that it might embarrass him: that he was strong enough without it. The movements proposed for Genl. Gibbon's column were carried out to the letter and had the attack been deferred until it was up I cannot doubt that we should have been successful. The Indians had evidently nerved themselves for a stand, but as I learn from Capt. Benteen, on the twenty-second, the cavalry marched twelve miles; on the twenty-third, thirty-five miles; from five A.M. till eight P.M. on the twenty-fourth, forty-five miles and then after night ten miles further; then after resting but without unsaddling, twenty-three miles to the battlefield. The proposed route was not taken but as soon as the trail was struck it was followed. I cannot learn that any examination of Tullock's creek was made. I do not tell you this to cast any reflection upon Custer. For whatever errors he may have commited he has paid the penalty and you cannot regret his loss more that I do, but I feel that our plan must have been successful had it been carried out, and I desire you to know the facts. In the action itself, so far as I can make out, Custer acted under a misapprehension. He thought, I am confident, that the Indians were running. For fear that they might get away he attacked without getting all his men up and divided his command so that they were beaten in detail. I do not at all propose to give the thing up here but I think that my troops require a little time and in view of the strength which the Indians have developed I propose to bring up what little reinforcement I can get. I should be glad of any that you can send me. I can take two companies of Infantry from Powder River and there are a few recruits and detached men whom I can get for the cavalry. I ought to have a larger mounted force than I now have but I fear cannot be obtained. I hear nothing from General Crook's operations. If I could hear I should be able to form plans for the future much more intelligently.

I should very much like instructions from you, or if not instructions, your views of the situation based as they might be on what has taken place elsewhere as well as here.

I shall refit as rapidly as possible and if at any time I should get information showing that I can act in conjunction with General Crook, or independently, with good results, I shall leave at once.

I send in another dispatch a copy of my written orders to Custer, but these were supplemented by the distinct understanding that Gibbon could get to the Little Big Horn before the evening of the 26th.

ALFRED H. TERRY
Brigadier General

14

Sir:

In obedience to verbal instructions received from you, I have the honor to report the operations of my battalion, consisting of Companies D, H, and K, on the 25th ultimo.

The directions I received from Lieutenant-Colonel Custer were, to move with my command to the left, to send well-mounted officers with about six men who would ride rapidly to a line of bluffs about five miles to our left and front, with instructions to report at once to me if anything of Indians could be seen from that point. I was to follow the movement of this detachment as rapidly as possible. Lieutenant Gibson was the officer selected, and I followed closely with the battalion, at times getting in advance of the detachment. The bluffs designated were gained, but nothing seen but other bluffs quite as large and precipitous as were before me. I kept on to these and the country was the same, there being no valley of any kind that I could see on any side. I had then gone about fully ten miles; the ground was terribly hard on horses, so I determined to carry out the other instructions, which were, that if in my judgment there was nothing to be seen of Indians, Valleys, &c., in the direction I was going, to return with the

---

NOTE: This and the following document (15) are the official reports of the battle, submitted by the two surviving battalion commanders. Captain Benteen made his report to Major Reno, through Lieutenant Wallace, the Regimental Adjutant. Major Reno then made his own report to General Terry, through Captain Smith who was the General's Adjutant.

battalion to the trail the command was following. I accordingly did so, reaching the trail just in advance of the pack-train. I pushed rapidly on, soon getting out of sight of the advance of the train, until reaching a morass, I halted to water the animals, who had been without water since about 8 P.M. of the day before. This watering did not occasion the loss of fifteen minutes, and when I was moving out the advance of the train commenced watering from that morass. I went at a slow trot until I came to a burning lodge with the dead body of an Indian in it on a scaffold. We did not halt. About a mile further on I met a sergeant of the regiment with orders from Lieutenant-Colonel Custer to the officer in charge of the rear-guard and train to bring it to the front with as great rapidity as was possible. Another mile on I met Trumpeter Morton [Martin], of my own company, with a written order from First Lieut. W. W. Cook to me, which read:

"Benteen, come on. Big village. Be quick. Bring packs. W. W. Cook."
"P. Bring Pac's."

I could then see no movement of any kind in any direction; a horse on the hill, riderless, being the only living thing I could see in my front. I inquired of the trumpeter what had been done, and he informed me that the Indians had "skedaddled," abandoning the village. Another mile and a half brought me in sight of the stream and plain in which were some of our dismounted men fighting, and Indians charging and recharging them in great numbers. The plain seemed to be alive with them. I then noticed our men in large numbers running for the bluffs on the right bank of the stream. I concluded at once that those had been repulsed, and was of the opinion that if I crossed the ford with my battalion, that I should have had it treated in like manner; for from long experience with cavalry, I judged there were 900 veteran Indians right there at that time, against which the large element of recruits in my battalion would stand no earthly chance as mounted men. I then moved up to the bluffs and reported my command to Maj. M. A. Reno. I did not return for the pack-train because I deemed it perfectly safe where it was, and we could defend it, had it been threatened, from our position on the bluffs; and another thing, it savored too much of coffee-cooling to return when I was sure a fight was progressing in the front, and deeming the train as safe without me.

Very respectfully,

F. W. BENTEEN
Captain Seventh Cavalry

Lieut. Geo. D. Wallace
Adjutant Seventh Cavalry

15

Headquarters 7th U.S. Cavalry,
Camp on Yellowstone River,
July 5th, 1876

Captain E. W. Smith
A.D.C. and A.A.A.G.

The command of the regiment having devolved upon me as the senior surviving officer from the battle of the 25th and 26th of June between the 7th Cavalry and Sitting Bull's band of hostile Sioux on the Little Big Horn River, I have the honor to submit the following report of its operations from the time of leaving the main column until the command was united in the vicinity of the Indian village.

The regiment left the camp at the mouth of the Rosebud river after passing in review before the Department Commander under command of Brevet Major General G. A. Custer, Lieutenant Colonel, on the afternoon of the 22nd of June and marched up the Rosebud twelve miles and encamped; – 23d marched up the Rosebud passing many old Indian camps and following a very large lodge-pole trail, but not fresh making thirty-three (33) miles; 24th the march was continued up the Rosebud, the trail and signs freshening with every mile until we had made twenty-eight (28) miles, and we then encamped and waited for information from the scouts; at 9-25 p.m. Custer called the officers together and informed us that beyond a doubt the village was in the valley of the Little Big Horn, and in order to reach it, it was necessary to cross the divide between the Rosebud and the Little Big Horn, and it would be impossible to do so in the day time without discovering our march to the Indians; that we would prepare to march at 11 p.m.; this was done, the line of march turning from the Rosebud to the right up one of its branches which headed near the summit of the divide. About 2 a.m. of the 25th the scouts told him that he could not cross the divide before daylight. We then made coffee and rested for three hours, at the expiration of which time the march was resumed, the divide crossed and about 8 a.m. the command was in the valley of one of the branches of the Little Big Horn; by this time Indians had been seen and it was certain that we could not surprise them and it was determined to move at once to the attack. Previous to this no division of the regiment had been made since the order had been issued on the Yellowstone annulling wing and battalion organization, but Custer informed me that he would assign commands on the march.

I was ordered by Lieutenant W. W. Cook Adjutant, to assume command of companies M, A, and G; Captain Benteen of companies H, D, and K, Custer retained C, E, F, I, and L under his immediate command and company B, Captain McDougall, in rear of the pack train.

I assumed command of the companies assigned to me and without any definite orders moved forward with the rest of the column and well to its left. I saw Benteen moving further to the left and as they passed he told me he had orders to move well to the left and sweep everything before him. I did not see him again until about 2-30 p.m. The command moved down the creek towards the Little Big Horn valley, Custer with five companies on the right bank, myself and three companies on the left bank and Benteen farther to the left and out of sight. As we approached a deserted village, and in which was standing one tepee, about 11 a.m.

43

Custer motioned me to cross to him, which I did, and moved nearer to his column until about 12-30 a.m. [p.m.] when Lieutenant Cook, Adjutant, came to me and said the village was only two miles ahead and running away; to move forward at as rapid a gait as prudent and to charge afterwards, and that the whole outfit would support me. I think those were his exact words. I at once took a fast trot and moved down about two miles where I came to a ford of the river. I crossed immediately and halted about ten minutes or less to gather the battalion, sending word to Custer that I had everything in front of me and that they were strong. I deployed and with the Ree scouts on my left charged down the valley driving the Indians with great ease for about 2½ miles. I however soon saw that I was being drawn into some trap as they would certainly fight harder and especially as we were nearing their village, which was still standing, besides I could not see Custer or any other support and at the same time the very earth seemed to grow Indians and they were running towards me in swarms and from all directions. I saw I must defend myself and give up the attack mounted. This I did, taking possession of a point of woods, and which furnished (near its edge) a shelter for the horses, dismounted and fought on foot. Making headway through the woods I soon found myself in the near vicinity of the village, saw that I was fighting odds of at least five to one and that my only hope was to get out of the woods where I would soon have been surrounded, and gain some ground. I accomplished this by mounting and charging the Indians between me and the bluffs on the opposite side of the river. In this charge 1st Lieutenant Donald McIntosh, 2nd Lieutenant Benj. H. Hodgson, 7th Cavalry and A.A. Surgeon J. M. DeWolf were killed. I succeeded in reaching the top of the bluff with a loss of three officers and twenty-nine enlisted men killed, and seven men wounded. Almost at the same time I reached the top, mounted men were seen to be coming towards us and it proved to be Colonel Benteen's battalion, companies H, D, and K. We joined forces and in a short time the pack train came up. As senior my command was then A, B, D, and G, H, K, M, and 380 men and the following officers, Captains Benteen, Weir, French, and McDougall, 1st Lieutenants Godfrey, Mathey, and Gibson, and 2nd Lieutenants Edgerly, Wallace, Varnum, and Hare and A. A. Surgeon Porter. 1st Lieutenant DeRudio was in the dismounted fight in the woods but having some trouble with his horse, did not join the command in the charge out, and hiding himself in the woods joined the command after night-fall of the 26th. Still hearing nothing of Custer and with this reinforcement, I moved down the river in the direction of the village, keeping on the bluffs. We heard firing in that direction and knew it could be only Custer. I moved to the summit of the highest bluff but seeing and hearing nothing, sent Capt. Weir with his company to open communications with him. He soon sent back word by Lieut. Hare that he could go no further and that the Indians were getting around him. At this time he was keeping up a heavy fire from his skirmish line. I at once turned everything back to the first position I had taken on the bluff and which to me the best. I dismounted the men and had the horses and mules of the pack train driven together in a depression, put the men on the crests of the hills making the depression and had hardly done so when I was furiously attacked, – this was about six p.m. We held our ground with a loss of eighteen enlisted men killed and forty-six wounded until the attack ceased about 9 p.m. As I knew by this time their overwhelming numbers and had given up any hope of support from that portion of the regiment with Custer, I had the men dig rifle pits; barricaded with dead horses and mules and boxes of hard bread the opening of the depression towards the Indians in which the animals were herded, and made every exertion to be ready for what I saw would be a terrific assault the next day. All this night the men were busy and the Indians holding a scalp dance underneath us in the bottom and in our hearing. On the morning of the 26th I felt confident that I could hold my own and was ready as far as I could be when at daylight about 2-30 a.m. I heard the crack of two rifles. This was the signal for the beginning of a fire that I have never seen equalled. Every rifle was handled by an expert and skilled marksman and with a range that exceeded our carbine, and it was simply impossible to show any part of the body before it was struck. We could see as the day brightened, countless hordes of them pouring up the valley from out of the village, and scampering over the high points towards the places designated for them by their chiefs and which entirely surrounded our position. They had sufficient numbers to completely encircle us, and the men were fighting all the Sioux nation, and also all the desperadoes, rene-gades, half-breeds, and squawmen between the Missouri and the Arkansas and east of the Rocky Mountains, and they must have numbered at least twenty-five hundred warriors. The fire did not slacken until about 9-30 a.m. and then we found they were making a last desperate effort and which was directed against the lines held by companies H, and M. In this charge they came close enough to use their bows and arrows, and one man lying dead within our lines was touched with the coup stick of one of the foremost Indians. When I say the stick was only twelve feet long, some idea of the desperate and reckless fighting of these people may be understood. This charge of theirs was gallantly repulsed by the men on that line led by Colonel Benteen. They also came close enough to send their arrows into the line held by Co's. D, and K, but were driven away by a like charge of the line which I accomplished. We now had many wounded and the question of water was vital, as from 6 p.m. of the previous evening until near 10 a.m., about 16 hours, we had been without.

A skirmish line was formed under Colonel Benteen to protect the descent of volunteers down the hill in front of his position to reach the water. We succeeded in getting some canteens although many of the men were hit in doing so. The fury of the attack was now over, and to our astonishment the Indians were seen going in parties toward the Village. But two solutions occured to us for this movement, that they were going for something to eat, more ammunition (as they had been throwing arrows) or that Custer was coming. We took advantage of this lull to fill all vessels with water, and soon had it by camp kettles full. But they continued to withdraw and all firing ceased soon; [except] occasional shots from sharp-shooters sent to annoy us about the water. About 2 p.m. the grass in the bottom was set on fire and followed up by Indians who encouraged its burning, and it was evident to me it was done for a purpose, and which purpose I discovered later on, to be the creation of a dense cloud of smoke behind which they were packing and preparing to move their village. It was between six and seven p.m. that the village came out behind the dense clouds of smoke and dust. We had a close and good view of them as they filed away in the direction of Big Horn mountains, moving in almost perfect military order. The length of the column was fully equal to that of a large division of the Cavalry Corps of the Army of the Potomac as I have seen it in its march.

We now thought of Custer, of whom nothing had been seen and nothing heard since the firing in his direction about six p.m. on the eve of the 25th, and we concluded that the Indians had gotten [between] him and us, and driven him towards the boat at the mouth of the Little Big Horn River. The awful fate that did befall him never occured to any of us as within the limits of possibility.

During the night I changed my position in order to secure an unlimited supply of water and was prepared for their return, feeling sure they would do so, as they were in such numbers; but early in the morning of the 27th and while we were on the *qui vive* for Indians, I saw with my glass a dust some distance down the valley. There was no certainty for some time what they were, but finally I satisfied myself they were cavalry, and if so could only be Custer, as it was ahead of the time that I understood that General Terry could be expected. Before this time however, I had written a communication to General Terry and three volunteers were to try and reach him. I had no confidence in the Indians with me and could not get them to do anything. If this dust were Indians, it was possible they would not expect anyone to leave. The men started and were told to go as near as it was safe to determine whether the approaching column was white men, and to return at once in case they found it so; but if they were Indians to push on to General Terry. In a short time we saw them returning over the high bluffs already alluded to. They were accompanied by a scout who had a note from Terry to Custer, saying Crow scouts had come to camp saying he had been whipped but that it was not believed. I think it was about 10-30 a.m. that the fate of General Custer and his brave men was soon determined by the dead bodies of many of their men: General G. Custer; Col. W. W. Cook, Adjutant; Captains M. W. Keogh, G. W. Yates, and T. W. Custer; 1st Lieuts. A. E. Smith, James Calhoun; 2nd Lieutenants W. V. Reilly of the 7th Cavalry, and J. J. Crittenden of the 20th Infantry, temporarily attached to this regiment. The bodies of Lieutenant J. E. Porter and 2nd Lieutenants H. M. Harrington and J. G. Sturgis, 7th Cavalry and Assistant Surgeon G. W. Lord, U.S.A. were not recognized, but there is every reasonable probability they were killed. It was certain that the column of five companies with Custer had been killed.

The wounded in my lines were during the afternoon and eve of the 27th, moved to the camp of General Terry, and 5 a.m. of the 28th I proceeded with the regiment to the battle ground of Custer and buried 204 bodies, including the following named citizens: Mr. Boston Custer, Mr. Reed (young nephew of General Custer), and Mr. Kellogg, a correspondent for the New York Herald. The following named citizens and Indians who were with my command were also killed: Charles Reynolds (guide and hunter); Isaiah Dorman (colored) interpreter; Bloody Knife who fell from immediately by my side; Bobtail Bull and Stab of the Indian scouts.

After traveling over his trail, it is evident to me that Custer intended to support me by moving further down the stream and attacking the village in the flank, that he

found the distance greater to the ford than he antic-
ipated; that he did charge, but his march had taken so
long, although his trail shows he had moved rapidly
that they were ready for him. That Co's. C, and I, and
perhaps part of E, crossed to the village or attempted it,
at the charge; were met by a staggering fire, and that
they fell back to find a position from which to defend
themselves, but they were followed too closely by the
Indians to permit time to form any kind of line. I think
had the regiment gone in a body, and from the woods
from which I fought advanced upon the village, its
destruction was certain. But he was fully confident they
were running away or he would not have turned from
me. I think (after the great number of Indians there
were in the village) that following reasons obtain for
the misfortune. His rapid marching for two days and
one night before the fight; attacking in the daytime at
12 M and when they were on the *qui vive* instead of
early in the morning, and lastly his unfortunate division of the regiment into three commands.

During my fight with the Indians I had the heartiest
support from the officers and men, but the conspicuous
service of Bvt. Col. F. W. Benteen, I desire to call attention to especially; for if ever a soldier deserved
recognition by his government for distinguished service, he certainly does. I enclose herewith his report of
the operations of his battalion from the time of leaving
the regiment until we joined commands on the hill. I
also enclose an accurate list of casualties as far as it can
be made at the present time, separating them into two
lists: "A", those killed in General Custer's command;
"B", those killed and wounded in the command I had.
The number of Indians killed can only be approx-
imated until we hear through the Agencies. I saw the

bodies of 18 and Captain Ball, 2d Cavalry, who made a scout of thirteen miles over their trail says that their graves were many along their line of march. It is simply impossible that numbers of them should not be hit in the several charges they made so close to my lines. They made their approaches through the deep gulches that led from the hill top to the river, and when the jealous care with which the Indian guards the bodies of killed and wounded is considered, it is not astonishing that their bodies were not found. It is probable that the stores left by them, and destroyed the next two days, was to make room for many on their travois. The harrowing sight of the dead bodies crowning the height on which Custer fell, and which will remain vividly in my memory until death, is too recent for me not to ask the good people of this country whether a policy that sets opposing parties in the field armed, clothed and equipped by one and the same government should not be abolished.

All of which is respectfully submitted.

M. A. RENO,
Major 7th Cavalry,
Com'd'g Regiment.

16

Fort Ellis, M. T.,
July 5th 1876

To the Asst Adjt Genl
Mil Div of the Mo   Chicago, Ills.

Sir:

I have the honor to inform you that on the afternoon of July 3d, '76 a scout, Taylor, arrived at this post from Genl. Terry's command with important dispatches for your headquarters.

I immediately in person took the dispatches to the telegraph office in Bozeman and was there informed that the line was in working order to Pleasant Valley.

On the 4th of July I went to town to see if the telegrams above referred to had been sent and found the telegraph office closed.

This afternoon on visiting Bozeman, I inquired if the telegrams left at the office on the 3d had been sent and was informed that they had been forwarded by mail this morning.

I deem this neglect of duty and criminal negligence on the part of the telegraph operator and report it accordingly.

If telegraph rates are charged on the dispatches above referred to between Bozeman and Helena, the bill should be repudiated and proceedings instituted against the company for neglect of duty because the dispatches were sent by mail from Bozeman to Helena, and if the agent had informed me that the telegrams

NOTE: This is the explanation from the commander of Fort Ellis for the delay in telegraphing General Terry's reports (Documents 12 and 13).

could not have been sent I could have forwarded them by courier and thereby have gained twenty four hours time.

Copies of telegrams above referred to are sent you by this mail.

I am, Genl   D. W. BENHAM,
Capt. 7th Inf. Comd'g. Post

17

Telegram

St. Paul, Minn.
8 July 1876

To the Ass't. Adjt. Gen.
Military Division of the Missouri;

The following just received:

Custer with his whole regiment & forty scouts and guides attacked an immense Indian village on the twenty-fifth & was defeated – have telegraphed particulars to Division Headquarters   The officers known to be killed are Gen'l Custer Captains Keogh Yates and Custer – Lieutenants Cook Smith McIntosh Calhoun Porter – Hodgson Sturgis and Reilly of the Cavalry Lieut Crittenden of the Twentieth Infantry & Acting Ass't Surgeon DeWolf Lieut Harrington & Ass't Surgeon Lord are Missing – Captain Benteen and Lieutenant Varnum are wounded but so slightly that they remain on duty – Mr Boston Custer the brother & Mr Reed the nephew of General Custer were killed – please telegraph to the commanding officers at Forts Lincoln & Rice to break the news to the families of the deceased officers & inform the commanding officer at Fort Totten of the death of DeWolf – please telegraph also to General Crittenden at Fort Abercrombie & to General Sturgis at St. Louis of the Death of their sons – inform Lieutenant Lord at Fort Snelling that his brother is missing – it is impossible as yet to determine the number

---

NOTE: This is the message General Terry sent to his own headquarters at St. Paul, Minnesota, via Captain Smith, being forwarded to General Sherman.

of killed but it must reach two hundred & fifty officers & men – there are fifty-one wounded – no other officers than those whom I have named were injured – It has been impossible as yet to obtain a nominal list of the killed & wounded among the enlisted men – Ask Division Headquarters for a copy of my dispatch.

ALFRED H. TERRY
Brig Gen'l

Please send me copy of Gen'l Terry's dispatch

RUGGLES
Ass't Adjt Gen

18

Headquarters Department of Dakota, in the Field
Camp on North Side of the Yellowstone River
near the Mouth of the Big Horn River,
July 9 1876

Gen'l George Crook
Comdg Department of the Platte, (in the field)

General,

On the 25th, ult. General Custer, crossing over from
the valley of the Rosebud to the Little Big Horn found
on the last named stream an enormous Indian Village.
He had with him his whole Regiment and a strong
detachment of scouts. At the time of the discovery of the
Indians he had but eight companies close at hand, but
with these he attacked in two detachments, one under
himself of five companies; the other under Major Reno,
of three companies. The attack of these detachments
were made at points nearly, if not quite, three miles
apart.

I greatly regret to say that Custer and every officer
and man under his immediate command, were killed.
Reno was driven back to the bluffs where he was joined
by the remainder of the Regiment. He was surrounded
by the enemy and was obliged to entrench himself, but
succeeded in maintaining himself in this position with
heavy loss until the appearance of General Gibbon's

NOTE: This letter was carried by Privates James Bell, Benjamin
Stewart, and William Evans of Company E, 7th Infantry. These men
left Colonel Gibbon's camp on July 9th and arrived at General
Crook's camp on July 12th. All three were commended in official
orders, and later received Congressional Medals of Honor.

command induced the Indians on the evening of the 26th. to withdraw.

Two hundred and sixty-eight officers, men, and civilians were killed and there are fifty-two wounded.

This affair occured about twenty miles above the junction of the Little Big Horn and the Big Horn. While Custer's column was in motion, Gibbon's column of about one hundred and fifty cavalry, one hundred and sixty Infantry and three Gatling Guns, was advancing to join Custer and co-operate with him in the attack upon the Indians. It was ferried across the Yellowstone at a point just below the mouth of the Big Horn, on the 24th. ultimo. On the 25th. it advanced through country of extreme difficulty, the Infantry twenty-two, the cavalry thirty-six miles. Custer had been informed that Gibbon's column would reach the mouth of the Little Big Horn on the evening of 26th. ultimo. Its advance was within four miles of that place at midnight of the 25th. ult. Reno's position was reached by Gibbon on the morning of the 27th. ult.

It is estimated that not less than twenty-four hundred warriors were in the fight. Beside the lodges in the village, a vast number of temporary shelters were found, showing that many Indians present there, besides those who properly belong to the village.

A reconnaisance southward was made on the 28th. ultimo and very large trail was found leading down the stream a distinct trail from the one (a heavy one) which Custer had followed from the Rosebud. Captain Ball, of the 2d Cavalry, who made this reconnaisance, was of the opinion that after leaving the valley the Indians divided into two bands, one making towards the mountains and the other towards the South and East.

It was a difficult task to get our wounded away, as the

character of the country had not permitted ambulances to accompany the troops and mule litters had to be made. They have now been sent back to Fort A. Lincoln.

In view of the shattered condition of the 7th. Cavalry and the damage done to our small pack-train, I have thought it best to bring the troops down to this depot to refit. I have sent for horses and mules for the dismounted men of the 7th. Cavalry, and for two more companies of Infantry.

I have twice tried to communicate with you but my scout each time has been driven back by Indians or rather reports that he was driven back. This morning I received from General Sheridan a copy of your dispatch to him, giving an account of your fight of the 17th. ultimo and as it gives me information of your position at that time, I hope that the bearers of this may be able to find your trail and reach you.

The great and, to me, wholly unexpected strength which the Indians have developed seems to me to make it important and indeed necessary that we should unite to at least act in close co-operation. In my ignorance of your present position and of the position of the Indians, I am unable to propose a plan for this, but if you will devise one and communicate it to me, I will follow it.

The boat which took down our wounded will, I hope, return with a supply of horses and mules with material for the repair of my saddles &c, and with some reenforcements.

I expect her back about the 16th. inst. and soon after that I hope to be able to move. I hope it is unnecessary for me to say that should our forces unite, even in my own Department, I shall assume nothing by reason of my seniority, but shall be prepared to co-operate with you in the most cordial and hearty manner, leaving you entirely free to pursue your own course. I am most anxious to assist you in any way that promise to bring the campaign to a favorable and speedy conclusion.

As my base of supplies is movable, (being a steamboat) I can start out from any point on the Yellowstone which may afford the readiest means of joining you and I think I shall be able to take with me from 15 to 20 days' rations on pack-saddles, though no forage. If, however, I should move up the Rosebud I could take a wagon train with me.

The following officers were killed on the 25th. ultimo: General Custer, Colonel Custer, Captain Keogh, Captain Yates, Lieutenants Hodgson, McIntosh, Cook, (Adjutant); A. E. Smith, Calhoun, Porter, Sturgis and Riley. Lieutenant Crittenden, 20th. Infantry, (attached to 7th. Cavalry), Assistant Surgeon Lord, A. A. Surgeon De Wolf   Lieut. Harrington missing.

Also Mr. Boston Custer and Mr. Reed, brother and nephew respectively of the General.

I am General, very truly yours,

ALFRED H. TERRY
Brigadier General

19

HeadQrs. 7th Cavalry
Camp on Yellowstone
July 11, 1876

Gen'l S. V. Benét
Chf. Ord. U.S.A.

I have the honor to report that in the engagement of the 25 and 26 of June 1876 between the 7th Cav & the hostile Sioux that out of 380 carbines in my command, six were rendered unserviceable in the following manner, (there were more rendered unservicable by being struck with bullets) failure of the breech block to close, leaving a space between the head of the cartridge & the end of the block, & when the piece was discharged, & the block thrown open, the head of the cartridge was pulled off & the cylinder remained in the chamber, where with the means at hand it was impossible to extract it. I believe this is a radical defect, & in the hands of hastily organized troops would lead to the most disastrous results. The defect results, in my opinion in two ways – in the manufacture of the gun the breech block is in many instances so made that it does not fit snug up to the head of the cartridge, after the cartridge is sent home, & it has always been a question in my mind whether the manner in which it revolves into its place does not render a close contact almost impossible to be made. Another reason is that the dust, always an element to be considered on the battlefield, prevents the

---

NOTE: The jamming of the carbines has often been pointed out by some to have been a major factor in Custer's defeat. Here is Major Reno's report to Brigadier General Stephen Vincent Benét, Chief of Ordnance, detailing the defects of the carbines in his command.

Head Qrs 7th Cavalry
Camp on Yellowstone
July 11 1876

Genl S.V. Benét
Chief Ord Dept

I have the
honor to report that in the engagement of the 25 & 26 of June
1876 between the 7th Cavy & the hostile
Sioux that out of 380 Carbines in my command
were rendered unserviceable in the
following manner, [these were
more rendered unserviceable
struck with bullet & bayonet & I
firmly believe an officer of that
regiment present with my command
the night of June 25th had he
would have given his right hand
for 50 bayonets, I had but 3
spades & 3 axes & with them loosened ground which the men threw
into piles in front of them with
tin cups & such other articles as
could in any way serve the same
purpose —

Very Resp'y
M A Reno
Maj 7th Cavy
Comdg Regt

PORTIONS OF THE FIRST AND FOURTH PAGES OF RENO'S REPORT ON THE CARBINES

786

ORDNANCE OFFICE FEB'Y JAN 29 1876

Headqurs Yellowstone

July 11th 1876

Maj. M. A. Reno

Report, suggests in charge of broch blocks in spring field &c. Carbines, Cal. 46, during late battles with the Sioux Indians

Lee 4528 —

2ª Endorsement

National Armory,
August 8 1876.

Respectfully returned to the Chief of Ordnance.

for Endorsement.

Ordnance Office,
War Department,
Washington July 30th 1876.

Respectfully referred to the Commanding Officer of National Armory.

J. G. Benét
Brig. Gen. Chief of Ordnance

ENDORSEMENTS OF RENO'S REPORT TO GENERAL BENÉT

proper closing of the breech block, & the same result is produced. There may be a want of uniformity in the flange of the head of the cartridge which would also render the action of the extractor null, altho' when the shell was left in the chamber the head would not be torn off.

I also observed another bad fault of the system altho' it did not render the guns unservicable, viz, the weight of the breech block is such that the hinges on which it revolves is very soon loosened, giving to the block a lateral motion, that prevents its closing.

I can also state that the blowing up of the breech block was a contingency that was patent to members of the Board which adopted the system & induced strong opposition to it, in the part of a minority. I send you these observations made during a most terrific battle, under circumstances which would induce men to fire with recklessness, as one's capture was certain death & torture, & the men fully appreciated the result of falling into the hands of the indians, & were not as cool perhaps as they would have been fighting a civilized foe. An indian scout who was with that portion of the Regt. which Custer took into battle, in relating what he saw in that part of the battle, says that from his hiding place he could see the men sitting down under fire & working at their guns, a story that finds confirmation in the fact that officers, who afterwards examined the battlefield, as they were burying the dead, found knives with broken blades lying near the dead bodies.

I also desire to call attention to the fact, that my loss would have been less had I been provided with some instrument similar to the "Trowel bayonet," & I am sure had an opponent of that arm been present with my command on the night of June 25th, he would have

given his right hand for 50 bayonets, I had but 3 spades
& 3 axes & with them loosened ground which the men
threw into piles in front of them with tin cups & such
other articles as could in any way serve this same purpose.

    Very Resp'y   M. A. RENO
                                              Maj. 7th Cav'y.
                                               Cmdg. Regt.

20

Headquarters U.S. Military Station
Standing Rock, D.T.
July 14, 1876

To the
Assistant Adjutant General
Department of Dakota
Saint Paul, Minn.

Sir:

For the information of the Hon. Secretary of War I respectfully report the following items of fact.

Ex Indian Agent Edmond Palmer in 1874 reported six thousand four hundred and forty 6440 indians at this agency.

I was stationed here during the winter and spring of 74 & 75 while Palmer was agent. I was frequently informed by parties who knew the indians intimately that there were not 4500 indians at this agency.

Agent John Burke relieved Palmer May 1st 75. In his Burkes Annual Official Report for 1875 among other absolute falsehoods, to which I have (February 1876) apparently uselessly called the attention of the proper authorities of the Government as this notorious liar through the malign influence of the church or the Devil or possibly the Beef Contractor – still holds a responsible government position despite the order of his excellency the President for his removal last March. –) Burke reports over 7000 indians that is to say as the Indian Agent's generally delight to reckon seven (7) souls to a lodge – there were over 1000 lodges at Standing Rock Agency.

NOTE: The above and the following report (Document 21) from the Indian Agency at Standing Rock, Dakota Territory, show some of the mismanagement that was alleged on the part of the Indian Agents.

It has been patent to residents here for months that young men were leaving and the number of arms in the possession of indians were disappearing very perceptibly since the departure of the troops for the Yellowstone Country.

I determined to count the lodges here and I now report the actual number within a radius of several miles. There are less than 300. Two hundred and ninety six 296, to which may be added perhaps fifty 50 more which are legitemately engaged in hunting game and who may possibly return without joining the hostiles. These lodges will not average over if as many as (5) five souls. There are not here now 1500 fifteen hundred indians.

There never has been for any considerable length of time forty five hundred indians at the Agency since its removal from Grand River to this point, and each and every report to the contrary was made knowingly and with the fraudulent intent, in my judgement, of procuring, and profiting by the secret and unauthorized sale of, surplus rations and annuities – and beef largesses.

The Indians here admit that half their numbers are out! hunting scalps as revealed by the massacre of June 25" 1876.

I respectfully assert without fear of error or contradictory proof that this agency – by reason of a system of starvation instituted about December 75 and the untamed malevolence of the Indian disposition has furnished 1500 fifteen hundred warriors armed with the best improved Henry and Winchester rifles each supplied with probably 100 one hundred rounds of ammunition per man – who are now enrolled among Sitting Bull's forces. Rations are issued here to the representatives of nine, 9 well known chiefs who are, beyond all doubt on the war path with the greater portion of their bands.

Starvation and predisposition led Kill Eagle chief of the Blackfeet Sioux with about twenty 20 lodges to go into the hostile camp. He alone it is said carried 3000 rounds of ammunition with him.

If each of the Sioux Agencies has furnished levies to the hostiles in proportion to this, Sitting Bull has 12000 warriors. But the population of the Sioux Nation is rated at an average of 28 twenty eight thousand. Estimating the entire fighting force at one fourth of the total, Sitting Bull has 7000 warriors.

Or again if the Indian population of each Sioux Agency has been overestimated in the same proportion as at Standing Rock D.T. which proportion is double the Actual number living here, and it is not improbable as E:G: "Gall" is rated here as a chief with 20 twenty lodges and at the same time as a chief with 100 one hundred lodges at Fort Peck Agency, you may safely infer that there are about 25 000 Sioux west of the Missouri River taking for the available fighting force one fourth I am prepared to assert that – while Sitting Bull has not had over 500 lodges at any time in the bands under him who have never consented and have never come into an Agency – yet by accessions and [illegible] received from the Sioux Agencies his force now exceeds 6 000 even the estimate of 1/5 for the fighting force will give him 5 000.

I respectfully add that Sitting Bull has as aides and special advisors five (5) renegade white men – one a spaniard – another a discharged soldier named Milburn from the 22nd Infantry who has been with him for several years. Milburn was once employed at Spotted Tail Agency as mail carrier under the alias of Charles Mimet. The Spaniard is well known at Ft.

Berthold Agency. The names of the three others I have not been able to learn. What I have stated herein can be I believe most fully substantiated in any court of justice.

The stand made by the Indians on the 25th of June would seem to confirm my estimate of the numbers under Sitting Bull, Black Moon, Gall et al. It has occurred to me that as soon as they find our force to be large enough to crush them, they will disintegrate into many smaller but still effective bodies. Some to raid posts ranches lines of travel others to return to their former homes the Agencies, Provision should be made for all such [illegible] but no effective plan can be maintained successfully until the entire control of Indian Affairs is turned over to an Authority powerful enough to command respect and obedience.

Permit me to mention one fact in connection with the Indians at this Agency. They have been *starved* for six weeks or two months and are entitled to consideration for not having all left for the prairies where they might at least have procured meat. Eighteen months supplies were sent here in 1875 and before the expiration of 14 fourteen months, these people were starving For six months they have received less or not more than half rations. This can also be established in a court of justice.

Having performed as I deem it an imperative duty to the military and the few good Indians at this Agency

I subscribe myself   Very Truly Your Obedt. Svt.

J. S. POLAND
Captain 6 Infy   Bvt Lt Col USA
Cmdg Post

1ST ENDORSEMENT

Headqrs. Dept. of Dakota,
St. Paul. Minn., July 24, 1876.

Respectfully forwarded to *Headquarters Military*

Division of the Missouri for the information of the
Lieutenant General.   GEO. D. RUGGLES
Asst. Adjt. Genl.
In the absence of the
Dept. Cmdr.

2ND ENDORSEMENT
Headqrs. Mil. Div. Mo.
Chicago, Aug. 11, 1876.
Respectfully forwarded.

There may be a great deal of truth in this communication, but if so, the bitterness exhibited by Capt. Poland renders it too doubtful to act upon.

I believe that Burke is unfitted for the position of
Agent, and have arranged so that Lieut. Col. Carlin
shall take the place of Capt. Poland, and the Secretary
of the Interior has promised to remove Burke.

Capt. Poland proves himself in error in his statistics
by saying that 1,500 warriors have left the Agency,
which would make, on his basis of one warrior to five
souls, 7,500 men, women and children belonging to the
Agency; whereas he states that there has never been at
the Agency over 4,500; and as there are now there at
least 1500 friendly, I do not see where he can get his
1500 warriors.   P. H. SHERIDAN
Lieut. General
Commanding

3RD ENDORSEMENT
Headquarters of the Army
Washington Aug. 16, 1876
Respectfully submitted to the *Secretary of War* in
connection with papers on this subject submitted on the
15th instant.   W. T. SHERMAN
General

21

Headquarters U. S. Military Station
Standing Rock, D.T., July 24, 1876.

To the Assistant Adjutant General
Department of Dakota,
Saint Paul, Minn.

Sir:

I respectfully report the following as having been
derived from seven Sioux Indians just returned from
the hostile camp (July 21st) some of whom were engaged in the battle of June 25th with the Seventh
Cavalry.

The agent of course makes no distinction between
them and the other Indians at the agency. He sent *them*
word to keep quiet and say nothing. To the other Indians he sent or delivered personally the instruction
they must not tell the military of the return of Indians
from the hostile camp, nor circulate reports of operations in the late fight.

The Indian account is as follows: The hostiles were
celebrating their greatest of religous festivals – the sun
dance – when runners brought news of the approach of
cavalry. The dance was suspended and a general rush –
mistaken by Custer, perhaps, for a retreat – for horses,
equipments and arms followed. Major Reno first attacked the village at the south end and across the Little
Big Horn. Their narrative of Reno's operations coincides with the published accounts: how he was quickly
confronted, surrounded; how he dismounted, rallied in

Note: This report of July 24 may be the first recorded version of the
Indians' side of the battle.

the timber, remounted and cut his way back over the ford and up the bluffs with considerable loss; and the continuation of the fight for some little time, when runners arrived from the north end of the village, or camp, with the news that the cavalry had attacked the north end of the same – three or four miles distant. The Indians about Reno had not before this the slightest intimation of fighting at any other point. A force large enough to prevent Reno from assuming the offensive was left and the surplus available force flew to the other end of the camp, where, finding the Indians there successfully driving Custer before them, instead of uniting with them, they separated into two parties and moved around the flanks of his cavalry. They report that he crossed the river, but only succeded in reaching the edge of the Indian camp. After he was driven to the bluffs the fight lasted perhaps an hour. Indians have no hours of the day, and the time cannot be given approximately.

They report that a small number of cavalry broke through the line of Indians in their rear and escaped, but was overtaken, within a distance of five or six miles, and killed. I infer from this that this body of retreating cavalry was probably led by the missing officers, and that they tried to escape only after Custer fell. The last man that was killed, was killed by two sons of a Santee Indian, "Red-top," who was a leader in the Minnesota massacre of '62 and '63.

After the battle the squaws entered the field to plunder and mutilate the dead. A general rejoicing was indulged in, and a distribution of arms and ammunition hurriedly made. Then, the attack on Major Reno was vigorously renewed. Up to this attack, the Indians had lost comparatively few men, but now, they say, their most serious loss took place.

They give no idea of numbers, but say there were a great great many. Sitting Bull was neither killed nor personally engaged in the fight. He remained in the council tent directing operations. Crazy Horse (with a large band) and Black Moon were the principal leaders on the 25th of June.

Kill Eagle, Chief of the Blackfeet, at the head of some twenty lodges left this agency about the last of May. He was prominently engaged in the battle of June 25, and afterwards upbraided Sitting Bull for not taking an active personal part in the engagement. Kill Eagle has sent me word that he was forced into this fight; that he desires to return to the agency; and that he will return to the agency if he is killed for it. He is reported actually on the way back to go to his white father the agent and make confession; to receive absolution for his defiant crime against the hand that has gratuitously fed him for three years. He is truly a shrewd chief, who must have discovered that he who fights and runs away may live to fight another day.

The Indians were not all engaged at any one time; heavy reserves were held to repair losses and renew attacks successively. The fight continued until the third day when runner kept purposely on the lookout, hurried in to camp and reported a great body of troops (General Terry's column) advancing up the river.

Lodges having been previously prepared for a move, a retreat, in a southerly direction, followed, towards and along the base of the Rosebud mountains. They marched about fifty miles, went into camp and held a consultation, where it was determined to send into all

the agencies reports of their success and to call upon
them to come out and share the glories that were to be
expected in the future. Wherefore, we may expect an
influx of overbearing and impudent Indians to urge, by
force perhaps, an accession to Sitting Bull's demands.

There is a general gathering in the hostile camp from
each of the agencies on the Missouri River, Red Cloud
and Spotted Tail's, as also a great many Northern
Cheyennes and Arapahoes (lila ota – a great many).

They report, for the especial benefit of their relatives
here, that in the three (3) fights they have had with the
whites they captured over 400 stand of arms – carbines
and rifles (revolvers not counted) – and ammunition
without end; some sugar, coffee, bacon and hard bread.
They claim to have captured, from the whites, this
summer, over 900 horses and mules. I suppose this in-
cludes operations against soldiers, Crow Indians and
Black Hills miners.

The general outline of this Indian report coincides
with the published reports. The first attack of Reno's
began well on in the day, say the Indians. They report
about 300 whites killed. They do not say how many
Indians were killed.

A report from another source says the Indians obtained from Custer's command 592 carbine and revolvers.

I have, since writing the above, heard the following
from the returned hostiles: They communicated, as a
secret to their particular friends here, the information
that a large party of Sioux and Cheyennes were to leave
Rosebud mountains, or the hostile camp, for this
agency, to intimidate and compel the Indians here to
join Sitting Bull; and if they refused, they are ordered

to soldier them (beat them) and steal their ponies. Of course any resistance to their attempts by the military or whites will provoke an attack upon the post, although that secret, or so much of it, has not been revealed to friends of the military.

I shall report any additional news received from reliable Indian sources as soon as obtained.

Very respectfully,   Your obedient servant,

J. S. POLAND
Captain 6th Infantry,
Brevet Lieut. Col. U.S.A.
Commanding.

22

Camp near Big Horn
on Yellowstone River,
July 4th, 1876

To his
Excellency the President
and the Honorable Representatives
of the United States.

Gentlemen:

We the enlisted men the survivors of the battle on the heights of Little Big Horn River, on the 25th and 26th of June 1876, of the 7th Regiment of Cavalry who sub-scribe our names to this petition, most earnestly solicit the President and Representatives of our Country, that the vacancies among the Commissioned Officers of our Regiment, made by the slaughter of our brave, heroic, now lamented Lieutenant Colonel George A. Custer, and the other noble dead Commissioned Officers of our Regiment who fell close by him on the bloody field, daring the savage demons to the last, be filled by the Officers of the Regiment only. That Major M. A. Reno, be our Lieutenant Colonel vice Custer, killed; Captain F. W. Benteen our Major vice Reno, promoted. The other vacancies to be filled by Officers of the Regiment

NOTE: This petition was drawn up and circulated by First Sergeant Joseph McCurry of Captain Benteen's company. The petition has been proven to have been "padded" with the names of soldiers dis-charged in May, deserters, and several outright forgeries. The petition traveled up through the various levels of official channels to General of the Army Sherman. After General Sherman added his endorsement (Document 23), the petition was returned to the Seventh Cavalry via General Townsend, the Adjutant General (see Document 24).

by seniority. Your petitioners know this to be contrary to the established rule of promotion, but prayerfully solicit a deviation from the usual rule in this case, as it will be conferring a bravely fought for and a justly merited promotion on officers who by their bravery, coolness and decision on the 25th and 26th of June 1876, saved the lives of every man now living of the 7th Cavalry who paticipated in the battle, one of the most bloody on record and one that would have ended with the loss of life of every officer and enlisted man on the field only for the position taken by Major Reno, which we held with bitter tenacity against fearful odds to the last.

To support this assertion – had our position been taken 100 yards back from the brink of the heights overlooking the river we would have been entirely cut off from water; and from behind those heights the Indian demons would have swarmed in hundreds picking off our men by detail, and before mid-day June 26th not an officer or enlisted man of our Regiment would have been left to tell of our dreadful fates as we then would have been completely surrounded.

With prayerful hope that our petitions be granted, we have the honor to forward it through our Commanding Officer.

Very Respectfully
(236 signatures)

23

Headquarters Army of the United States,
Washington, D.C.
August 5, 1876.

The judicious and skilful conduct of Major Reno and
Captain Benteen is appreciated, but the promotions
caused by General Custer's death have been made by
the President and confirmed by the Senate; therefore
this petition cannot granted. When the Sioux campaign
is over I shall be most happy to recognize the valuable
services of both officers and men by granting favors or
recommending actual promotion.

Promotion on the field of battle was Napoleon's fa-
vorite method of stimulating his officers and soldiers to
deeds of heroism, but it is impossible in our service
because commissions can only be granted by the President on the advice and consent of the Senate, and
except in original vacancies, promotion in a regiment is
generally if not always made on the rule of seniority.

W. T. SHERMAN,
General.

24

Headquarters of the Army,
Adjutant General's Office,
Washington, August 10, 1876.

Major M. A. Reno
7th Cavalry
(Through Headquarters Military Division
    of the Missouri)

Sir:

Referring to the petition of the enlisted men of the 7th Cavalry (forwarded by you the 15th ultimo) for the promotion of yourself and other officers of the regiment who participated in the engagement of June 25, 1876, I have the honor to enclose herewith, for the information of the officers and enlisted men concerned, a copy of the remarks of the General of the Army with reference to the request contained in the petition.

Very respectfully,   Your obedient Servant

E. D. TOWNSEND,
Adjutant General.

25

Headquarters District of Montana,
Fort Shaw, Montana, October 17, 1876.

Sir: I have the honor to submit the following report of the military operations of the troops under my
command during the last spring and summer:

In accordance with telegraphic instruction from the
brigadier general commanding the department, five
companies of the Seventh Infantry left Fort Shaw on
the 17th of March, and proceeded toward Fort Ellis.

The ground was covered with heavy snow and the
roads a mass of mud and slush, but the command made
good time and reached Fort Ellis on the 28th, a distance
of 183 miles. In the mean time, one company of the
Seventh (Clifford's) had been ordered to march from
Camp Baker, and the snow being too deep on the direct
road to Fort Ellis, Captain Clifford dug his way
through snow-drifts to the Missouri River and reached
Fort Ellis on the 22d of March. From that point he was
instructed by telegraph to proceed as an escort to our
supply-train as far as the new Crow agency.

The battalion of the Seventh Infantry from Fort
Shaw, under command of Captain Freeman, left Fort
Ellis on the 30th of March, and the 1st of April the
four companies of the Second Cavalry left the post
under command of Captain Thompson. Major Brisbin,
although on crutches from rheumatism, and unable to

Note: Colonel Gibbon submitted this extensive report of the operations of his command to General Terry, via Major Ruggles who was
the Adjutant for the Department of Dakota, after the summer's campaigns were completed.

mount a horse, insisted so strongly upon accompanying the expedition that I consented to his going, although he was obliged to travel in an ambulance.

The road over the divide, between Fort Ellis and the Yellowstone River, was in an almost impassable condition, and to add to our difficulties a furious snow-storm set in on the 3d of April, and it was midnight on the 4th before our train succeeded in getting across and reaching Shields River, a distance of thirty miles. From there the cavalry and wagon-train was pushed down the river after the infantry, fording the Yellowstone twice, and overtook Captain Freeman's command in camp on the river opposite the new agency on the 7th. On the 8th I proceeded to the agency, 18 miles, held a council with the Crows the next day, and the day after (10th) enlisted 25 of them as scouts. Lieutenant Jacobs having arrived with wagons, our supplies were loaded up to transfer them to the north bank of the Yellowstone.

Clifford's company having left the agency the day before, (9th) on the 11th the train was started in a furious snow-storm which had raged all night, and pulling for a part of the way through snow two feet deep, reached the point selected for our depot; the command in the mean time having marched there.

Having established the supply camp, and left "A" company (Logan's) in charge of it, the command resumed the march down the river on the 13th. The ground, however, was very soft, and our heavily-loaded wagons made but slow progress, but after fording the Yellowstone four times we reached the vicinity of Fort Pease on the 20th. The next day I received a dispatch from the department commander to proceed no further than the mouth of the Big Horn for the present, and placed the command alongside of Fort Pease. On the

23d, Captain Freeman's company was sent back with the wagontrain to bring up the supplies; and on the 24th Captain Ball, with two companies of the Second Cavalry, was started on a scout to old Fort C. F. Smith. He returned by the way of the Little Big Horn and Tullock's Fork on the 1st of May without having seen any signs of Indians. Captain Freeman, with Logan's company and our train, got back on the 8th of May, and on the 10th the march down the river was resumed with the consolidated command, and all our supplies in the train.

Up to the 3d of May we had seen no sign of Indians, but on the morning of that day the ponies of the Crow scouts, which had been carelessly permitted to roam at large, were found to be missing, together with two animals belonging to one of our guides, and signs demonstrated the fact that a war party had been in our vicinity.

On the 14th we went into camp near the Little Porcupine, (Table Creek of Lewis and Clarke,) where we were visited by a terrific storm of hail and rain which rendered the prairies impassable for our wagons and detained us till the 20th. Scouts had been sent out constantly, not only on the north side toward the mouth of Tongue River, but on the south side of the Yellowstone. These reported seeing various war parties of Sioux, and finally the smoke of a camp on the Rosebud about thirty-five miles from us. With the design of striking this camp and surprising it by a night march, I attempted to cross the Yellowstone on the 17th, but that river had become a rapid torrent, and after drowning four of our horses in attempting to get them across, the effort was abandoned. On the 20th, our scouts having reported a large body of Indians moving toward the mouth of the Rosebud with an evident design of cross-ing the Yellowstone, I moved with the whole of the command, except Kirtland's company, hastily down the river and camped for the night below the mouth of the Rosebud, but saw no Indians, and the next day brought Captain Kirtland's company and the train down to the new position.

On the 23rd Lieutenant English, with I Company, Seventh Infantry, and Lieutenant Roe's Company F, Second Cavalry, to accompany it a part of the way, was started back to meet and escort in a contract-train, bringing us supplies from Fort Ellis. The morning the escort left (23d) two soldiers and a citizen teamster, while hunting in the hills a few miles from camp, were murdered by Indians, who, however, rapidly disap-peared before a scouting party of two companies, under Captain Ball, sent after them. On the 27th I started a dispatch for the department commander down the river in a small boat in charge of Privates Evans and Stewart, Company E, Seventh Infantry, and Scout Williamson, the two soldiers having volunteered for the service; and the next day I received the department commander's dispatch of the 15th instant, directing me to march at once for the stockade above Glendive Creek, cross the Yellowstone, and move out east-ward to meet him. Cap-tain Sanno, Seventh Infantry, with two companies his own and Lieutenant Roe's, Second Cavalry – was at once started, with all our wagons under charge of Lieu-tenant Jacobs, regimental quartermaster Seventh In-fantry, back to lighten the contract-train and hurry it forward; and on the 4th of June it reached camp after a rapid march in spite of a furious storm of snow and sleet, which raged all day on the 1st. The next day (5th) the march was resumed down the river, but we were delayed by steep hills and rugged country, and in four days made only 57 miles, which brought us about 17 miles below the mouth of Tongue River. That night (8th) I received by scouts the department commander's dispatch of that day from Powder River, and the next morning met him on the steamboat Far West a few miles below our camp. In accordance with his instructions the command was at once prepared to move up the river again, but a furious rain-storm that afternoon delayed the movement by converting the alkali flats surrounding us into impassable ground. The cavalry, however, got off on the afternoon of the 10th and infantry the next day, and after a march of 50 miles was again concentrated in camp below the mouth of the Rosebud on the 14th. On the 18th Major Reno, with a force of cavalry, arrived opposite our camp after a scout on Powder, Tongue, and Rosebud Rivers, during which he reported he had seen no Indians, and the next day he proceeded down the river.

A cavalry scout up the river having reported the side streams almost impassable, by reason of floods from recent rains, I started Captain Freeman with three companies of infantry on the 21st, up the road to build bridges. General reaching the camp by steamer shortly afterward, the whole command was started up the river. I, at his request, accompanied him on the Far West, for the purpose of conferring with Lieutenant-Colonel Custer, who reached a point on the opposite side of the river with the whole of the Seventh Cavalry that afternoon.

That evening the plan of operations was agreed upon. Lieutenant-Colonel Custer, with the Seventh Cavalry, was to proceed up the Rosebud till he struck an Indian trail, discovered during Major Reno's scout. As my scouts had recently reported smoke on the Little Big Horn, the presence of an Indian camp some distance up that stream was inferred.

Lieutenant-Colonel Custer was instructed to keep constantly feeling toward his left, well up toward the mountains, so as to prevent the Indians escaping in that direction, and to strike the Little Big Horn, if possible, above (south of) the supposed location of the camp, while my command was to march up the Yellowstone to the mouth of the Big Horn, there to be ferried across by the steamer, then to move up the Big Horn to the mouth of the Little Big Horn, and up that stream, with the hope of getting the camp between the two forces. As it would take my command three days to reach the mouth of the Big Horn, and probably a day to cross it over the Yellowstone, besides two more to reach the mouth of the Little Big Horn, and Lieutenant-Colonel Custer had the shorter line over which to operate the department commander strongly impressed upon him the propriety of not pressing his march too rapidly. He got off with his regiment at 12 o'clock the next day, (22d) three gatling guns, under Lieutenant Low, Twentieth Infantry, being detached from his regiment and sent to join my command. The steamer got away at 4 o'clock that day, and reached Fort Pease early on the morning of the 24th. My command except the train and Captain Kirtland's company, (B, Seventh Infantry,) being at once ferried across, was that evening, moved out to the crossing of Tullock's Fork. I did not accompany it and General Terry took command of the troops in person. The next day the steamer entered the mouth of the Big Horn and proceeded up that stream.

The next morning early, (26th,) I left the Far West and overtook the infantry portion of the command,

General Terry having made a night march with the
cavalry and Gatling guns, and later in the day that portion of the command was overtaken on a high ridge
overlooking the valley of the Little Big Horn near its
mouth, where by direction of General Terry, I resumed
command of my troops. Shortly afterward our scouts
brought in news that they had encountered some Indians, and, giving chase had run them across the Big
Horn. They had dropped articles in their flight which
proved them to be Crows, assigned to duty with Lieutenant-Colonel Custer's command. They, having discovered that their pursuers belonged to their own tribe,
refused to come back, and called across the river that
Custer's command had been entirely destroyed by the
Sioux, who were chasing the soldiers all over the country and killing them. We now pushed up the valley of
the Little Big Horn as rapidly as the men could march,
large fires being seen in the distance. Efforts were made
to communicate with Lieutenant-Colonel Custer by
scouts, but our Crow interpreter deserted and took the
Crows with him, and two attempts made by white men
to precede the command with dispatches failed, the
scouts in both cases running into Indians. As we proceeded up the valley the fires increased in number and
volume, giving rise to the impression that Custer had
captured the camp and destroyed it. The Indians, who
late in the afternoon appeared in sight on the hills in
front of us, rather militated against the supposition,
however and after marching until dark we halted and
bivouaced on the prairie.

The next morning the march was resumed, and after
proceeding about 3 miles we came in sight of a large
deserted Indian camp, in which two teepies were still
standing, and these were found to contain the dead

bodies of Indians. Many lodge poles were still standing, and the quantity of property scattered about testified to the hasty departure of the Indians. Our scouts reported only a few scattering horsemen in sight on the distant hills. We continued to move rapidly forward, still uncertain as to the fate of Custer's command, Captain Ball's company about a mile in advance. While passing through the Indian camp a report reached me from our scouts in the hills to the north of the river that a large number of bodies of white men had been discovered, and shortly afterward Lieutenant Bradley came in with the information that he had counted 194 bodies of dead soldiers. All doubt that a serious disaster had happened to Lieutenant-Colonel Custer's command now vanished, and the march was continued under the uncertainty as to whether we were going to rescue the survivors or to battle with the enemy who had annihilated him. At length we caught sight of a number of animals congregated upon the slope of distant hill, and on a point nearer to us three horsemen were evidently watching us. After Captain Ball's company had passed them these cautiously approached us, our troops being convinced we were friends, they came forward more rapidly and announced that the Seventh Cavalry had been cut to pieces and the remnant, under Major Reno, were intrenched in the bluffs close by. Communication was now soon opened with Major Reno. His command was found intrenched upon the tops of several small ridges, their dead and living horses lying about them, with some fifty wounded men lying on the hot, dusty hilltops, where, until about 6 o'clock on the evening before, they had been unable to obtain any water except at the imminent risk of life. We were informed that in this spot they had been surrounded by overwhelming numbers of Indians from the close of Major Reno's charge on the 25th (about 2½ p. m.) until about 6 p. m. the next day, the Indians pouring upon them all that time a very close and almost continuous fire from the neighboring ridges, some of which commanded the position in reverse. The first inquiry made was if General Custer was with us, and the command appeared to know nothing of the fate of himself and that portion of his command immediately with him until we informed them of it. As described to us, the whole movement of the Indians when they abandoned their camp was visible from Major Reno's position, and the last portion disappeared in the hills to the south just at dusk on the 26th, when my command was 8¾ miles from Major Reno's position.

My command was at once placed in camp, and the arrangements made to bring down and properly care for the suffering wounded. This was effected by night-fall. The next day, 28th, Captain Ball, Second Cavalry, was sent out with his company, and followed the main trail some ten or twelve miles. We found that it led directly south toward the Big Horn Mountains, and in returning to camp he discovered a large fresh trail leading down the Little Big Horn toward the scene of the battle. The day was occupied in burying the dead and in constructing litters for the wounded. In the performance of the latter duty Lieut. G. C. Doane, Second Cavalry, was detailed to devise mule-litters, and, with the very crudest material, (cottonwood poles, raw-hide, and ropes,) made some six or eight. But the mules, when attached to them, proved so intractable that the attempt was abandoned, and hand-litters of lodge-poles and canvas constructed. With these, and the men to carry them, the command left camp at sunset on that day. The movement, however, was exceedingly slow and tedious. The whole command, afterward assisted by two companies of the Seventh Cavalry, was used by relays, and it was long past midnight when camp was reached, at a distance of four and one-half miles.

The next day (20th) was occupied in destroying the large quantity of property abandoned by the Indians in their hasty flight. An immense number of lodge-poles, robes, and dressed skins, pots, kettles, cups, pans, axes, and shovels, were found scattered through the camp and along the trail followed by the Indians. Our progress with the hand-litters having proved so exceedingly slow and tedious Lieutenant Doane was called upon to continue the construction of the mule-litters, and by selecting from all the pack-mules in the command he succeeded in obtaining fifty gentle enough for the service, and in constructing a sufficient number of litters to carry all the wounded. With these a second start was made at 6 p. m., with the expectation of making a short march. But the litters worked so admirably as to call forth the most unbounded commendation in praise of the skill and energy displayed by Lieutenant Doane, and after proceeding a few miles information was received by courier that the Far West was waiting for us at the mouth of the Little Big Horn. The department commander therefore decided to continue the march with the view of placing the wounded in comfort and rest as soon as possible. The march was then resumed, but the night proved dark and stormy and road down from the plateau to the steamer rough and obscure, so that it was two o'clock on the morning of the 30th before the wounded were safely housed on board the boat. This was done without a single accident of any moment, and I desire to invite special attention to the invaluable services of Lieutenant Doane in the construction of the requisite litters in so short a time out of the rude material of clumsy poles, horse raw-hide, and refractory mules. But for his energy, skill, and confidence our suffering wounded would probably have been several days longer on the road.

The Far West left that day for the mouth of the Big Horn, which point I reached with the command, after a two day's march, on the 2d of July. The whole command was then ferried across the Yellowstone River and placed in camp. Here it remained until the 27th, when, in obedience to the orders of General Terry, it was transferred down the river to the new depot at the mouth of the Rosebud, and on the 3d of August my portion of it was ferried across the Yellowstone, preparatory to the movement up the Rosebud.

The troops in the field were now re-organized, and I was assigned to the command of the four battalions of infantry belonging to the Fifth, Sixth, Seventh, and Twenty-second Infantry. On the 8th the command started up the Rosebud, but the road was difficult, required a great deal of work, and our progress was slow.

On the 10th we encountered General Crook's command coming down, and the next day the united commands started with pack-mules on the Indian trail which General Crook was following, the battalion of the Fifth Infantry being sent back to escort our supply-train and scout the river to prevent the Indians crossing to the north of it. In the midst of very heavy rain the command moved across to Tongue River, down that and across to Powder River, and down that to its mouth, which was reached on the 17th. On the 25th my command, further reduced by the detachment of the Sixth Infantry, started up Powder River again, but the following day, on information that the Indians were below us, on the Yellowstone, we retraced our steps, and marched across the country to a point on the River near O'Fallon's Creek, and the day following, 27th, were ferried across the Yellowstone by steamer. That night the whole command made a night-march to the north, entering upon an almost entirely unknown country without guides, where, for the next four days, our movements were hampered by the necessity for marching toward the water pools, which had to be first sought for. Our general course, however, was northward, and scouting parties sent across the main divide and down the Yellowstone having demonstrated that no large bodies of Indians had made their way north, toward the Fort Peck agency, the command came in again to the Yellowstone, near Glendive Creek on the 31st.

On the 5th of September I received orders for my Command to return to its station in Montana.

Starting on the 6th, we reached our wagon-train a few miles above the mouth of Powder River, 81 miles, on the 9th, and placing our pack-mules in harness, resumed the march the next day. On the 13th we reached the mouth of Tongue River, and on the 17th passed Fort Pease. On our arrival at the mouth of Big Timber, on the 26th, the command was divided, the cavalry companies under Captain Ball marching to Fort Ellis, and the infantry to Camp Baker, via the forks of the Muscleshell. The cavalry reached Fort Ellis on the 29th of September, and the five companies of the Seventh Infantry arrived at Fort Shaw on the 6th instant, having left Company E (Clifford's) at Camp Baker on the 2d. I preceded the cavalry into Ellis, and, having arranged for the muster-out and payment of the Crow scouts, returned to this post on the 4th instant.

It gives me great pleasure to testify to the cheerful manner in which the whole command performed the long marches and arduous duties of the campaign. Starting out in the depths of winter, with the expectation of an absence of two or three months, they submitted to the tedious delays, long marches, and exposures of an unprecedentedly wet and cold season during six months with a soldierly cheerfulness worthy of the highest praise.

In concluding this report I beg leave to submit the following suggestions:

It became evident during the campaign that we were attempting to carry on operations in an extensive region of something like four or five hundred miles square with inadequate means. Had we been called upon to operate against only the Indians known to be hostile, any one of the three columns sent against them would have been amply sufficient to cope with any force likely to be brought against it; but when the hostile body was largely re-enforced by accessions from the various agencies where the malcontents were doubtless in many cases driven to desperation by starvation and the heartless frauds perpetrated upon them, the problem became less simple, and when these various bands succeeded in finding a leader who possessed the tact, courage, and ability to concentrate and keep together so large a force, it was only a question of time as to when one or other of the exterior columns would meet with a check from the overwhelming numbers of the interior body. The first information we had of the force and strategy opposed to us was the check given to Custer's column, resulting in a disaster which might have been worse but for the timely arrival of General Terry's other column.

The inadequate means at the disposal of the troops became painfully apparent at an early day. Operating on one bank of a deep and rapid stream for a distance of several hundred miles, my column was entirely without the means of crossing to the other bank to strike exposed camps of the hostile bands.

Incumbered with heavily-loaded wagon-trains, our movements were necessarily slow, and when we did cut loose from these our only means of transporting supplies were the mules taken from the teams, and unbroken to packs, unsuitable pack-saddles, and inexperienced soldiers as packers. These latter soon learned to do their part tolerably well, but at the expense of the poor animals, whose festering sores after a few days' marching appealed not only to feelings of humanity, but demonstrated the false economy of the course pursued.

At the end of one scout with pack-mules most of our animals had to be replaced by others from the train, and at the end of the campaign many of them were in anything but a serviceable condition for either pack or draught purposes. The contrast between the mobility of our force and that of General Crook's was very marked, especially for rapid movements. General Crook's well-organized pack-train, with trained mules and its corps of competent packers, moved almost independently of the column of troops, and as fast as they could move. His ranks were not depleted by drafts to take charge of the packs and animals, for each mule faithfully followed the sound of the leader's bell and needed no other guide, and his pack-mules were neither worn out nor torn to pieces by bad saddles and worse packing.

In addition to our other wants, we were entirely devoid of any proper means for the transportation of sick or wounded. This, with a well-organized pack-train, was comparatively easy. As it was, a few wounded men were all-sufficient to cripple, for offensive operations, a large body of troops; for in savage warfare to leave one's wounded behind is out of the question.

Maps of the route passed over by the command will be forwarded as soon as they can be completed. The country visited by the troops is by no means the desert it has been frequently represented. There is, of course, a great deal of barren, worthless land, but there is also much land in the valleys susceptible of cultivation, and an immense region of good grazing country which will in time be available for stock-raising. Even where from the valleys the appearance of the so-called "bad lands" was most forbidding, we found on the plateau above excellent grass in the greatest abundance covering the country for great distances. This was particularly noticeable in the region north of Powder River, between the Yellowstone and Missouri Rivers, and along the Tongue and Rosebud and the country between the two. The country along the Little Big Horn is also a fine grass country, and along the Big Horn itself immense valleys of fine grass extend.

During the summer's operations the cavalry marched nearly 1,500 miles, and the infantry nearly 1,700, besides some 900 miles by portions of the cavalry and 500 miles by portions of the infantry in scouting and escort duty.

I am, sir, very respectfully, your obedient servant,
JOHN GIBBON
Colonel Seventh Infantry,
Commanding District
Maj. Geo. D. Ruggles
Assistant Adjutant-General, Department of Dakota.

26

HEADQUARTERS DEPARTMENT OF DAKOTA
St. Paul Minn.
Dec. 9th 1876

General W. T. Sherman
Washington D.C.

I see that in your Annual Report you quote at length my dispatch from the Little Horn battlefield. That dispatch was so mangled by the telegraph, that in some places it is almost nonsense. In my Annual Report I give it as it was sent, and I respectfully request that the quotation in your report be corrected to correspond with the latter.

ALFRED H. TERRY
Brig. Gen'l.

NOTE: This letter of General Terry to General Sheridan requests some corrections in his official report for 1876, regarding the Battle of the Little Big Horn.

A CHRONOLOGICAL LIST OF BATTLES IN THE SIOUX-CHEYENNE CAMPAIGNS OF 1876

MARCH 5, 1876 – Supply camp on Dry Forks of Powder River, Wyoming. Capt. Edwin M. Coates, commanding companies C and I, 4th Infantry.

MARCH 17, 1876 – Indian Village on Little Powder River, Montana. Col. J. J. Reynolds, 3rd Cavalry, commanding companies E, I and K, 2nd Cavalry; and E, F and M, 3rd Cavalry.

JUNE 9, 1876 – Army camp on Tongue River, Wyoming. Brig. Gen. George Crook commanding companies A, B, D, E, and I, 2nd Cavalry; A, B, C, D, E, F, G, I, L and M, 3rd Cavalry; D and F, 4th Infantry; and C, G and H, 9th Infantry.

JUNE 17, 1876 – On Rosebud River, Montana. Brig. Gen. George Crook commanding companies A, B, D, E and I, 2nd Cavalry; A, B, D, E, F, G, I, L and M, 3rd Cavalry; D and F, 4th Infantry; and C, G and H, 9th Infantry.

JUNE 25 & 26, 1876 – Indian village on Little Big Horn River, Montana. Lt. Col. G. A. Custer, 7th Cavalry, commanding companies A, B, C, D, E, F, G, H, I, K, L and M, 7th Cavalry.

JULY 7, 1876 – At head of Tongue River, Montana. Second Lieut. F. W. Sibley, 2nd Cavalry, commanding detachment of twenty men of the 2nd Cavalry.

JULY 17, 1876 – Near Hat Creek, Wyoming. Col. Wesley Merritt, 5th Cavalry, commanding companies A, B, D, G, I, K and M, 5th Cavalry.

JULY 29, 1876 – Steamer "Carroll" at mouth of Powder River, Montana. Lt. Col. E. S. Otis, 22nd Infantry, commanding companies E, F, G, H, I and K, 22nd Infantry.

AUGUST 2, 1876 – Forage dump on Powder River, Montana. Maj. O. H. Moore, 6th Infantry, commanding companies D and I, 6th Infantry; and C, 17th Infantry.

AUGUST 23, 1876 – Steamers "Josephine" and "Benton" near mouth of Yellowstone River, Montana. First Lieut. Nelson Bronson, 6th Infantry, commanding Company G, 6th Infantry.

SEPTEMBER 9, 1876 – Indian Village at Slim Buttes, Dakota. Brig. Gen. George Crook commanding companies A, B, D, E and I, 2nd Cavalry; A, B, C, D, E, F, G, I, L and M, 3rd Cavalry; A, B, C, D, E, F, G, I, K and M, 5th Cavalry; D, F and G, 4th Infantry; C, G and H, 9th Infantry; and B, C, F and I, 14th Infantry.

SEPTEMBER 14, 1876 – Owl Creek, Dakota. Maj. J. J. Upham, 5th Cavalry, commanding detachment of 150 men of the 5th Cavalry.

OCTOBER 11, 1876 – Spring Creek, Montana. Capt. C. W. Miner, 22nd Infantry, commanding companies C, 17th Infantry; and G, H and K, 22nd Infantry.

OCTOBER 15 & 16, 1876 – Clear Creek, Montana. Lt. Col. E. S. Otis, 22nd Infantry, commanding companies C and G, 17th Infantry; and G, H and K, 22nd Infantry.

OCTOBER 21, 1876 – Cedar Creek, Montana. Col. N. A. Miles, 5th Infantry, commanding companies A, B, C, D, E, F, G, H, I and K, 5th Infantry.

OCTOBER 23, 1876 – Chadron Creek, Nebraska. Col. R. S. Mackenzie, 4th Cavalry, commanding companies B, D, E, F, I and M, 4th Cavalry; and H and L, 5th Cavalry.

OCTOBER 27, 1876 – Big Dry River, Montana. Col. N. A. Miles, 5th Infantry, commanding companies A, B, C, D, E, F, G, H, I and K, 5th Infantry.

NOVEMBER 25 & 26, 1876 – Bates Creek, Wyoming. Col. R. S. Mackenzie, 4th Cavalry, commanding companies K, 2nd Cavalry; H and K, 3rd Cavalry; B, D, E, F, I and M, 4th Cavalry; and H and L, 5th Cavalry.

DECEMBER 7, 1876 – Bark Creek, Montana. First Lieut. F. D. Baldwin, 5th Infantry, commanding companies G, H and I, 5th Infantry.

DECEMBER 18, 1876 – Red Water Creek, Dakota. First Lieut. F. D. Baldwin, 5th Infantry, commanding companies G, H and I, 5th Infantry.

**Officers and Troops
of the Campaign**

ABBREVIATIONS USED IN
COMMAND ROSTERS AND MUSTER ROLLS

AAAG   Acting Assistant Adjutant General, the staff officer in charge of keeping official records, correspondence, etc.

AAQM   Acting Assistant Quartermaster, the staff officer in charge of supplies, forage, and ammunition.

ACS   Acting Commissary of Subsistence, the staff officer in charge of food.

ADC   Aide-de-Camp

Bn   Battalion

CMO   Chief Medical Officer

D.S.   Detached Service away from the regiment

E.D.   Extra Duty for which the soldier received extra pay, such as teamster or laborer with the quartermaster or subsistence departments or as hospital nurse.

E.O.   Engineer Officer

IHCA   In Hands of Civil Authorities

Mtd. Det.   Mounted Detachment

O.O.   Ordnance Officer

PM   Paymaster

QMD   Quartermaster Department

RQM   Regimental Quartermaster

S.D.   Special Duty such as serving with the Mounted Detachment or the Gatling Gun crew.

Subs. Dept.   The Subsistence or Commissary department.

TDy   Temporary Duty other than the regularly assigned; an officer serving with another company than his own.

Contents of Command Rosters and Company Muster Rolls

COMMAND TABLES OF ORGANIZATION
Department of Dakota, Montana Column, June 1876.
Col. Gibbon
Department of the Platte, Column awaiting rein-
forcements at Camp Cloud Peak, June 20, 1876.
Gen. Crook
Department of the Missouri, Column to reinforce
the Department of the Platte, in the South Chey-
enne Valley. Col. Carr
Department of Dakota, Dakota Column. Gen. Terry

MUSTER ROLLS OF COMPANIES
IN THE BATTLE VICINITY
Seventh Infantry, under Col. Gibbon
Companies A, B, E, H, I, K
Second Cavalry, under Col. Gibbon
Companies F, G, H, L
Sixth Infantry, under Maj. Orlando H. Moore
Companies C, D, I
Twentieth Infantry, under Gen. Terry
Gatling Gun Detachment
Sixth Infantry, under Gen. Terry
Company B
Seventeenth Infantry, under Gen. Terry
Companies C, G
Seventh Cavalry, under Gen. Terry
Headquarters; Band; Companies A through M

Command Rosters

DEPARTMENT OF DAKOTA
Montana Column, June 1876

Col. John Gibbon, 7th Inf. (Brvt. Maj. Gen. USA)
1st Lt. Levi Frank Burnett, Adjt. 7th Inf. (Brvt. Capt. USA)
1st Lt. Joshua West Jacobs, RQM 7th Inf.
> Company A, 7th Infantry
>> Capt. William Logan
>> 1st Lt. Charles Austin Coolidge
>
> Company B, 7th Infantry
>> Capt. Thaddeus Sanford Kirtland
>> 2nd Lt. Charles Austin Booth
>
> Company E, 7th Infantry
>> Capt. Walter Clifford
>> 2nd Lt. George Schæffer Young
>
> Company H, 7th Infantry
>> Capt. Henry Blanchard Freeman (Brvt. Maj. USA)
>> 2nd Lt. Frederick Monroe Hill Kendrick
>
> Company I, 7th Infantry
>> 1st Lt. William L. English
>> 2nd Lt. Alfred Bainbridge Johnson
>
> Company K, 7th Infantry
>> Capt. James Madison Johnson Sanno
>> 2nd Lt. Charles Albert Woodruff
>
> Crow Indian Scouts & Mounted Detachment, 7th Infantry
>> 1st Lt. James Howard Bradley, Co. B, 7th Infantry

Maj. James Sanks Brisbin, 2nd Cav. (Brevt. Col. USA)
    Company F, 2nd Cavalry
        2nd Lt. Charles Francis Roe
    Company G, 2nd Cavalry
        Capt. James Nicholas Wheelan
        1st Lt. Gustavus Cheeny Doane
        2nd Lt. Edward John McClernand
    Company H, 2nd Cavalry
        Capt. Edward Ball
        1st Lt. James George McAdams
    Company L, 2nd Cavalry
        Capt. Lewis Thompson (Brvt. Maj. USA)
        1st Lt. Samuel Todd Hamilton
        2nd Lt. Charles Brewster Schofield

1st Lt. Holmes Offley Paulding, Ass't. Surg.

DEPARTMENT OF THE PLATTE
Column awaiting reinforcements
at Camp Cloud Peak
after the Battle of the Rosebud
June 20, 1876

Brig. Gen. George Crook, USA (Brvt. Maj. Gen. USA)
AAAG   1st Lt. John Gregory Bourke, Co. L, 3rd Cav.
ACS   1st Lt. John Wilson Bubb, Co. I, 4th Inf.
CMO   Capt. Albert Hartsuff, Ass't. Surg. (Brvt. Lieut.
        Col. USA)
ADC   2nd Lt. Walter Scribner Schuyler, Co. B, 5th
        Cav.

Crow & Shoshone Indian Scouts
    Capt. George Morton Randall, Co. I, 23rd Inf.
    (Brvt. Maj. USA)

CAVALRY COMMAND
Lt. Col. William Bedford Royall, 3rd Cav. (Brvt. Col.
USA)
AAAG   2nd Lt. Henry Rowan Lemly, Co. E, 3rd Cav.
AAQM   2nd Lt. Charles Morton, Co. A, 3rd Cav.

3RD CAVALRY
Maj. Andrew W. Evans, 3rd Cav. (Brvt. Lieut. Col.
USA)
Adjt.   2nd Lt. George Francis Chase, Co. L, 3rd Cav.
        Company A, 3rd Cavalry
            1st Lt. Joseph Lawson
        Company B, 3rd Cavalry
            Capt. Charles Meinhold

Company C, 3rd Cavalry
   Capt. Frederick Van Vleit (Brvt. Lieut. Col. USA)
Company D, 3rd Cavalry
   2nd Lt. James Ferdinand Simpson (Brvt. Capt. USA) (TDy from Co. B)
Company E, 3rd Cavalry
   Capt. Alexander Sutorius
   1st Lt. Adolphus H. Von Luettwitz (TDy from Co. C)
Company F, 3rd Cavalry
   2nd Lt. Bainbridge Reynolds
Company G, 3rd Cavalry
   1st Lt. Emmett Crawford
Company I, 3rd Cavalry
   Capt. William Howard Andrews
   2nd Lt. James E. H. Foster
Company L, 3rd Cavalry
   Capt. Peter Dumont Vroom
Company M, 3rd Cavalry
   Capt. Anson Mills (Brvt. Lieut. Col. USA)
   1st Lt. Augustus Choteau Paul
   2nd Lt. Frederick Schwatka

2ND CAVALRY BATTALION
Capt. Henry Erastus Noyes, Co. I, 2nd Cav. (Brvt. Maj. USA)
   Company A, 2nd Cavalry
   Capt. Thomas Bull Dewees
   2nd Lt. Daniel Crosby Pearson
Company B, 2nd Cavalry
   1st Lt. William Charles Rawolle
Company D, 2nd Cavalry
   1st Lt. Samuel Miller Swigert
   2nd Lt. Henry Dustan Huntington

Company E, 2nd Cavalry
    Capt. Elijah Revillo Wells (Brvt. Maj. USA)
    2nd Lt. Frederick William Sibley
Company I, 2nd Cavalry
    Capt. Noyes
    2nd Lt. Frederick William Kingsbury

INFANTRY COMMAND
Company D, 4th Infantry
    Capt. Avery Billings Cain (Brvt. Maj. USA)
Company G, 9th Infantry
    Capt. Thomas Bredin Burrowes (Brvt. Maj.
    USA)
    1st Lt. William Lewis Carpenter
Company H, 9th Infantry
    Capt. Andrew Sheridan Burt (Brvt. Maj.
    USA)
    2nd Lt. Edgar Brooks Robertson

Capt. Julius Herman Patzki, Ass't. Surg.

DEPARTMENT OF THE MISSOURI
Column ordered out as reinforcement
to the Department of the Platte
marching through the South Cheyenne valley, June 1876

Lt. Col. Eugene Asa Carr, 5th Cav. (Brvt. Maj. Gen. USA)
Maj. John Jacques Upham, 5th Cav.
1st Lt. William Curtis Forbush, Adjt. 5th Cav.
1st Lt. Charles Henry Rockwell, RQM 5th Cav.
> Company A, 5th Cavalry
> > Capt. Robert Phillips Wilson
> Company B, 5th Cavalry
> > Capt. Robert Hugh Montgomery
> Company C, 5th Cavalry
> > 2nd Lt. Edward Livingston Keyes
> Company D, 5th Cavalry
> > Capt. Samuel Storrow Sumner (Brvt. Maj. USA)
> > 1st Lt. Calbrith Perry Rodgers
> Company G, 5th Cavalry
> > Capt. Edward Mortimer Hayes
> > 2nd Lt. Hoel Smith Bishop
> Company I, 5th Cavalry
> > Capt. Sanford Cobb Kellogg (Brvt. Lieut. Col. USA)
> > 1st Lt. Bernard Reilly, Jr.
> Company K, 5th Cavalry
> > Capt. Julius Wilmot Mason (Brvt. Lieut. Col. USA)
> > 1st Lt. Charles King

Company M, 5th Cavalry
  Capt. Edward Henry Leib (Brvt. Lieut. Col.
    USA)
  2nd Lt. Charles Henry Watts

Company F, 19th Infantry
  Capt. Philip Halsey Remington
  2nd Lt. Cornelius Gardener

Maj. Thaddeus Harlan Stanton, PM

DEPARTMENT OF DAKOTA
Dakota Column

Brig. Gen. Alfred Howe Terry, USA (Brvt. Maj. Gen. USA)

AAAG Capt. Edward Worthington Smith, Co. G, 18th Inf. (Brvt. Lieut. Col. USA)

AAQM 1st Lt. Henry James Nowlan, RQM, 7th Cav.

ACS 2nd Lt. Richard Edward Thompson, Co. K, 6th Inf.

EO 1st Lt. Edward Maguire, Engineers

OO Capt. Otho Ernest Michaelis, Ordnance

CMO Capt. John Winfield Williams, Ass't. Surg. (Brvt. Maj. USA)

ADC Capt. Robert Patterson Hughes, Co. E, 3rd Inf. (Brvt. Maj. USA)

ADC 1st Lt. Eugene Beauharnais Gibbs, Co. C, 6th Inf.

Maj. Orlando Hurley Moore, 6th Inf., Cmdg.*
Company C, 6th Infantry
Capt. James W. Powell
2nd Lt. Bernard A. Byrne, Bn. ACS, AAQM

---

* NOTE: Major Moore's Companies C, D and I, 6th Infantry, left Fort Buford, D.T., May 14, 1876, aboard the steamer "Josephine," and arrived at Stanley's Crossing of the Yellowstone on May 18. Here this battalion maintained a supply camp. The companies were moved to the Supply Camp at the mouth of Powder River: Co. C on June 5, Co. I on June 10, and Co. D on June 12 via the steamer "Far West." On June 12, Companies C and G, 17th Infantry, from General Terry's column were added to Major Moore's command.

Company D, 6th Infantry
    Capt. Daniel H. Murdock
      1st Lt. Frederick W. Thibaut, Bn. Adjt.
Company I, 6th Infantry
    2nd Lt. George B. Walker

Gatling Gun Battery, 20th Infantry Detachment
    2nd Lt. William Hale Low, Jr., Co. C, 20th Inf.
    2nd Lt. Frank Xavier Kinzie, Co. F, 20th Inf.

Company B, 6th Infantry
    Capt. Stephen Baker
    1st Lt. John Carland

Company C, 17th Infantry
    Capt. Malcolm McArthur
    1st Lt. Frank Dillon Garretty
    2nd Lt. James Dallas Nickerson
Company G, 17th Infantry
    Capt. Louis H. Sanger (Brvt. Maj. USA)
    1st Lt. Josiah Chance
    2nd Lt. Henry Perrine Walker

Lt. Col. George Armstrong Custer, 7th Cav. (Brvt. Maj. Gen. USA)
Maj. Marcus Albert Reno, 7th Cav. (Brvt. Col. USA)
1st Lt. William Winer Cooke, Adjt. 7th Cav. (Brvt. Lt. Col. USA)
    Company A, 7th Cavalry
      Capt. Myles Moylan
        1st Lt. Charles Camilus De Rudio, TDy from Co. E, 7th Cav.
    Company B, 7th Cavalry
      Capt. Thomas Mower McDougall
      2nd Lt. Benjamin Hubert Hodgson

Company C, 7th Cavalry
    Capt. Thomas Ward Custer (Brvt. Lieut. Col.
    USA)
    2nd Lt. Henry Moore Harrington
Company D, 7th Cavalry
    Capt. Thomas Benton Weir (Brvt. Lieut. Col.
    USA)
    2nd Lt. Winfield Scott Edgerly
Company E, 7th Cavalry
    1st Lt. Algernon Emorey Smith, TDy from
    Co. A, 7th Cav. (Brvt. Capt. USA)
    2nd Lt. James Garland Sturgis, TDy from
    Co. M, 7th Cav.
Company F, 7th Cavalry
    Capt. George W. Yates
    2nd Lt. William Van Wyck Reily, TDy from
    Co. E, 7th Cav.
Company G, 7th Cavalry
    1st Lt. Donald McIntosh
    2nd Lt. George Daniel Wallace
Company H, 7th Cavalry
    Capt. Frederick William Benteen (Brvt. Col.
    USA)
    1st Lt. Francis Marion Gibson
Company I, 7th Cavalry
    Capt. Myles Walter Keogh (Brvt. Lieut. Col.
    USA)
    1st Lt. James Ezekiel Porter
Company K, 7th Cavalry
    1st Lt. Edward Settle Godfrey
    2nd Lt. Luther Rector Hare
Company L, 7th Cavalry
    1st Lt. James Calhoun, TDy from Co. C, 7th
    Cav.

2nd Lt. John Jordan Crittenden, TDy from Co. G, 20th Inf.

Company M, 7th Cavalry

Capt. Thomas Henry French

1st Lt. Edward Gustave Mathey

Arikara Indian Scout Detachment

2nd Lt. Charles Albert Varnum, Co. A, 7th Cav.

1st Lt. George Edwin Lord, Ass't. Surg.

Company Muster Rolls

SEVENTH INFANTRY
COMPANY A

Capt. William Logan	Cmdg. Co.
1st Lt. Charles A. Coolidge	
1st Sgt. John Rafferty	
Sgt. Patrick Rogan	At Ft. Shaw, for duty
Sgt. Samuel Plant	
Sgt. Richard B. Dickinson	
Sgt. George C. Meysel	At old Ft. Pease, sick
Cpl. Paul Daniels	
Cpl. James Randall	S.D. w/Gatling Gun
Cpl. Adolph Heinzman	
Cpl. Christian Sipfler	At old Ft. Pease
Musc. John McLennon	
Musc. Henry McNary	At Ft. Shaw, for duty
Artif. Joseph Klewitz	At old Ft. Pease, E.D. w/QMD
Pvt. Charles Alberts	At old Ft. Pease, E.D. w/QMD
Lorenzo D. Brown	
August Brethauer	At Ft. Shaw, dischgd. 5 May 1876
John Cannon	At Ft. Shaw, for duty
George W. Cullom	
James Doyle	At old Ft. Pease, E.D. w/QMD
James Drew	
James E. Goodwin	S.D. w/Mtd. Detach.
Thomas Harrington	
Levi Heider	
George Leher	
James C. Lehmer	

Pvt. Lemuel Loomis   At Ft. Shaw, for duty
     Michael J. McCabe   At Ft. Shaw, sick
     William MacBeth   At Ft. Leavenworth,
                              dishon. dischgd.
                              15 May 1876
     John C. Martin
     William Moore   At old Ft. Pease, E.D.
                              w/QMD
     Carl Pilts   At Col. Gibbon's HQ
                              w/pioneer party
     John G. Pfenniger   At Ft. Shaw, for duty
     Morris C. Roche   S.D. w/Gatling Gun
     Joseph Smith
     John B. Smith
     Patrick Sullivan
     Edward Stumpf
     William H. Thompson   At Ft. Ellis, sick
     James Walsh   S.D. w/Mtd. Detach.
     William Walter
     James Collins

Temporarily attached for duty at Fort Shaw 9 Mar
1876:
     Pvt. William H. Aubrey   Co. G
          John J. Conner   Co. G
          Isaac H. Spayd   Co. G
          Frank McCollum   Co. F   At old Ft. Pease

A part of Capt. Freeman's battalion of the command
accompanying Brig. Gen. Terry, Company A had two
officers and twenty-three men. 2nd Lt. Francis Wood-
bridge was appointed 29 Feb. 1876 and not yet reported.

SEVENTH INFANTRY
COMPANY B

Capt. Thaddeus S. Kirtland — Cmdg. Co.

1st Lt. James H. Bradley — Cmdg. Mtd. Detach.

2nd Lt. Charles A. Booth

1st Sgt. John Cashman

Sgt. Leroy H. Dayton — At old Ft. Pease, dischgd. 31 May 1876

Sgt. Michil Lauls — At Ft. Ellis, dischgd. 16 June 1876

Sgt. William Wolchert

Sgt. Henry E. Schreiner — Act. Comsy. Sgt. attached to Co. K, 7th Inf.

Cpl. Henry Smith

Cpl. George Jabowing

Cpl. William A. Short — At Ft. Shaw, for duty

Cpl. Thomas Baiggo

Musc. Philip Reid

Pvt. John Baaer

John O. Bennett — At old Ft. Pease, E.D. w/QMD

Herbert Clark

Patrick Coakly

Alfred DeGroot

Augustus W. Ford

Frank Geiger

Frederick Groshan

Frank E. Hastings

William Hinkler

William Ickler

Pvt. Albert Kifer	S.D. w/Mtd. Detach.
James Knox	
John Madden	S.D. w/Mtd. Detach.
George F. Meakings	At Chicago, Ill., for duty as clerk
John Miller	
Edward Mulcahy	
Edgar W. Parker	
Edward Poetling	
Martin Reap	
Gelbert Roseboon	At Ft. Shaw, for duty
Joseph C. Sinsil	At old Ft. Pease, E.D. w/QMD
Louis Striber	
Sylvester Waltz	
James A. Watson	At old Ft. Pease, E.D. w/QMD
August Weber	
Benjamin F. Williams	At Ft. Shaw, for duty

Temporarily attached for duty at Ft. Shaw 9 Mar. 1876:

Pvt. Frank McHugh	Co. G
James Norton	Co. G
Edward Welsh	Co. G

A part of Capt. Freeman's battalion, Company B was at old Fort Pease with two officers and thirty-one men. First Lt. Bradley was commanding the Mounted Detachment and Indian Scouts.

SEVENTH INFANTRY
COMPANY E

Capt. Walter Clifford	Cmdg. Co.
2nd Lt. George S. Young	
1st Sgt. Peter T. R. Van Ardenne	
Sgt. Samuel Bellow	At Camp Baker, for duty
Sgt. James Bell	
Sgt. Daniel Dommitt	
Sgt. George W. Jaques	At Camp Baker, for duty
Cpl. Collomb Spalding	
Cpl. William Wright	
Cpl. John C. Clark	
Cpl. William D. Bendell	Promoted Cpl. 7 May 1876
Musc. George C. Beary	
Musc. John Rafferty	
Pvt. William Atkinson	Confined Camp Baker 18 June 1875
Charles A. Barker	
James Bell	
John Burns	
Matthew Butterly	
John Duane	
Matthias Efferts	
William Evans	
William Funk	Reduced from Cpl. 3 May 1876
Charles Grady	Confined IHCA 8 Dec. 1875
William Gray	Confined IHCA 14 Mar. 1876

Pvt. Henry Heiner	At Camp Baker, dischgd. 5 May 1876
William Hensley	
August Hickman	At Ft. Columbus, N.Y., waiting transport
Francis Honicker	
Lewis G. Hubbard	
John Miller	
Vincent McKenna	
James McKibben	
Thomas Mullen	At Camp Baker, for duty
William Noonan	
Thomas O'Malley	
Frederick A. Rapp	At Camp Baker, for duty
August Raw	
Walter S. Robertson	
William H. Sanders	
Thomas Scott	
Benjamin F. Stewart	
James M. Thomas	At Camp Baker, dischgd. 29 Mar. 1876
Samuel Wallace	
George W. Wood	

Temporarily attached for duty at Camp Baker 14 Mar. 1876:

Sgt. Lewis G. Einbaum	Co. D	At old Ft. Pease
Sgt. Riley R. Lane	Co. D	
Pvt. John Howard	Co. D	
Robert F. Williams	Co. D	E.D. as hospital attendant

A part of Capt. Freeman's battalion of the command accompanying Brig. Gen. Terry, Company E had two officers and thirty-five men. First Lt. William I. Reed was on Detached Service at Camp Baker.

SEVENTH INFANTRY
COMPANY H

Capt. Henry B. Freeman   Cmdg. Co. & Bn.
2nd Lt. Frederick M. H. Kendrick
1st Sgt. George G. Howard
Sgt. John M. Glengell   At Ft. Shaw, for duty
Sgt. Charles R. Hill
Sgt. George Stein
Sgt. Edward M. Ferguson
Cpl. William Moran
Cpl. Eugene Navarra
Cpl. Patrick Rudden
Cpl. James Costello
Musc. Francis Rein
Musc. Robert L. Cosgrove   At Ft. Shaw, for duty
Pvt. Joseph Barkman
    Joseph Biddle
    William Bolts
    John H. Buskirk
    Robert Copely
    Thomas Curran
    Patrick J. Finigan
    Augustus Freiberg
    Eugene Grant
    Henry S. Groff   S.D. w/Mtd. Detach.
    Elijah Hall
    Albert H. Jones
    Peter Lorentzen
    Thomas Martin
    George Matthews
    Martin Millet

Pvt. Michael Partridge
 James Reader
 George Rivers
 Henry Rice   S.D. w/Mtd. Detach.
 Albert Ross
 Henry Scott
 Archy T. Segman
 George Von Thianich At old Ft. Pease, E.D.
           w/QMD

 Charles Walters
 William West
 George F. Woodard
 William H. Woodhouse
 Frank Wolf
 Peter Young   At old Ft. Pease, E.D.
           w/QMD

Temporarily attached for duty at Ft. Shaw 9 Mar. 1876:
 Pvt. William D. Mathews Co. G
 Frank B. Morton   Co. G At old Ft. Pease

A part of Capt. Freeman's battalion of the command accompanying Brig. Gen. Terry, Company H had two officers and thirty-six men. First Lt. William H. Nelson was absent sick at Fort Shaw.

SEVENTH INFANTRY
COMPANY I

1st Lt. William L. English   Cmdg. Co.
2nd Lt. Alfred B. Johnson
1st Sgt. Thomas H. Wilson
Sgt. Milden H. Wilson
Sgt. Michael Rigney   On steamer "Far West,"
    sick

Sgt. Patrick Bosquill
Sgt. Michael Hogan
Cpl. Charles Bishop
Cpl. George A. Wolfe
Cpl. John L. Reynolds
Cpl. Richard M. Cunliffe
Musc. Robert Gilbert   At Ft. Shaw, for duty
Pvt. Charles P. Arden   At Ft. Shaw, for duty
    John Bane
    James Bell
    William Carson   At old Ft. Pease, E.D.
    w/QMD

    Thomas Collins
    Lewis Chaplin
    Gustav Eishorn   At Ft. Shaw, dischgd.
    5 May 1876

    Patrick Fallon
    Thomas Frost
    Moses W. Gebhard   At Ft. Shaw, for duty
    Henry W. Gray
    Maurice Keating   Confined Ft. Shaw
    Charles J. Keegan
    William Louett
    Edward Linehau

Pvt. Charles Meinhart	At Ft. Shaw, for duty
Peter Moan	
Nicholas Murphy	
Richard Orrington	
Thomas Ralph	
William Roller	s.d. w/Mtd. Detach.
Patrick Scanlon	
Henry Scott	At Ft. Shaw, for duty
Walter Selden	
Calvin Smith	
Joseph B. Stivers	At Ft. Shaw, for duty
Peter Tenni	
William Thompson	
James Wilhight	
Thomas Wilkinson	

Temporarily attached for duty at Ft. Shaw 9 Mar. 1876:

Cpl. William Baker	Co. G	At old Ft. Pease
Pvt. Holmes L. Coon	Co. G	
Charles Heinze	Co. G	
Martin Sullivan	Co. G	s.d. w/Mtd. Detach.

A part of Capt. Freeman's battalion of the command accompanying Brig. Gen. Terry, Company I had two officers and thirty-one men. Capt. Charles C. Rawn was absent sick at Fort Shaw.

SEVENTH INFANTRY
COMPANY K

Capt. James M. J. Sanno	Cmdg. Co.
2nd Lt. Charles A. Woodruff	Battal. Adjt. & Cmdg. Gatling Gun
1st Sgt. Walter E. Garlock	
Sgt. Thomas F. Stanford	
Sgt. Louis Hines	At old Ft. Pease, sick
Sgt. William J. Wilson	
Sgt. James E. Moran	At old Ft. Pease, E.D. w/QMD
Cpl. Thomas Cox	At old Ft. Pease, dischgd. 5 May 1876
Cpl. James D. Abbott	S.D. w/Mtd. Detach.
Cpl. Frederick Stortz	S.D. w/Gatling Gun
Musc. Herman Wendling	
Artif. John Kleis	
Artif. Charles W. Fannin	At old Ft. Pease, E.D. w/QMD
Pvt. James Allen	At Ft. Shaw, for duty
August W. Bender	S.D. w/Gatling Gun
Thomas J. Bishop	At Ft. Shaw, dischgd. 12 June 1876
Howard Clark	
Orison C. Cochran	
Peter H. Conniff	
Peter W. Frost	At old Ft. Pease, E.D. w/QMD
Joseph Gallagher	
Jacob Goldberg	Confined in the field 17 Apr. 1876
David Heaton	S.D. w/Mtd. Metach.

Pvt. Lummen W. Hoffman	S.D. w/Gatling Gun
Philo O. Hurlburt	At old Ft. Pease, sick
Charles Keating	
Robert Marlow	
William MacIntosh	S.D. w/Mtd. Detach.
James McFarland	
Frederick Meyer	At old Ft. Pease
Frank Murphy	S.D. w/Gatling Gun
Edwin L. Perkins	At Ft. Shaw, dishon. dischgd. 20 Apr. 1876
Noah G. Pomeroy	
George Rogers	At old Ft. Pease
Joseph Sanford	
William Simon	
Richard Smith	At Ft. Shaw, for duty
Michael Stritten	

Temporarily attached for duty at Ft. Shaw 9 Mar. 1876:

Sgt. Joseph L. Farrell	Co. G	S.D. w/Mtd. Detach.
Pvt. Michael Fogarty	Co. G	
Robert M. Isgrigg	Co. G	S.D. w/Mtd. Detach.
John Meier	Co. G	

Specially attached by verbal order of Capt. Freeman:

Sgt. Henry E. Schwinn	Co. B, 7th Inf., Actg. Comsy. Sgt.
Sgt. Charles Becker	Co. D, Bn. of Engs.
1st Cl. Pvt. Joseph Weis	Co. D, Bn. of Engs.

A part of Capt. Freeman's battalion of the command accompanying Brig. Gen. Terry, Company K had one officer and eighteen men. First Lt. Allan H. Jackson was on Detached Service at Washington, D.C., since 26 May 1875, and 2nd Lt. Woodruff was battalion Adjutant and commanding the Gatling Gun.

SECOND CAVALRY
COMPANY F

2nd Lt. Charles F. Roe	Cmdg. Co.
1st Sgt. Alexander Anderson	
Sgt. John R. Nelson	
Sgt. Thomas Wallace	
Sgt. William Leipler	
Sgt. Richard Davis	
Sgt. John H. Sarven	
Cpl. Edward G. Granville	
Cpl. Ausburn B. Conklin	Escorting mail to Ft. Ellis
Cpl. E. Dwight Chapman	
Trumpet. William C. Osmer	
Blksm. Joseph Baker	
Far. William J. Cleeland	
Sad. Thomas Jones	
Pvt. Frederick Allen	
George H. Barnes	At old Ft. Pease, E.D. w/QMD
Claus Brummer	At Ft. Ellis, for duty
William Burke	
Benjamin Betts	
James Bovard	E.D. as hospital attendant
Andrew Brouse	At Ft. Ellis, sick
Thomas Carroll	
Marion Childers	At Ft. Ellis, for duty
John Craden	At Ft. Ellis, for duty
Robert H. Cowen	
Michael Cowley	

Pvt. John E. Duggan
James Farrell
Thomas Graham
Frank Glackewsky
Edward Harrington
Charles E. Hall
John W. Jones
Christie Kaiser
Charles A. Lauthammer
Charles Leslie   Escorting mail to Ft.
                        Ellis
John McLaughlin
George W. M.   At Ft. Sanders, for duty
  Merryman   (Drum-Major)
David Melvill
John G. Moore
John J. O'Flynn
John O'Sullivan
Adolf Puryear
William S. Parker
Daniel C. Starr
George Schick   At Ft. Ellis, for duty
George H. Sibbeske
George Shuless
Oliver Shaw   At Ft. Ellis, for duty
William F. Somers
Charles Sweeny   Confined Ft. Ellis
Edward Seibert
Thomas Turnholt
Henry Watson
Joseph Waller
George S. Wall
William H. White

Pvt. Alonzo Wilfert	At Ft. Ellis, for duty
Johan Youk	Escorting mail to Ft. Ellis

A part of Major Brisbin's battalion of the Command accompanying Brig. Gen. Terry, Company F had one officer and forty-five men. Capt. George L. Tyler was on Detached Service at Ft. Ellis since 1 Apr. 1876 and 1st Lt. Frank C. Grugan was on Detached Service with the Office of the Chief Signal Officer, Washington, D.C., since 19 Aug. 1873. See pages 83-84 regarding Col. Gibbon's absence on the day of the battle.

SECOND CAVALRY
COMPANY G

Capt. James N. Wheelan	Cmdg. Co.
1st Lt. Gustavus C. Doane	
2nd Lt. Edward J. McClernand	Actg. Eng. Off., Col. Gibbon's staff
1st Sgt. George E. Barnaby	
Sgt. Asher Davey	At Ft. Ellis, for duty
Sgt. George W. Prentice	
Sgt. Andrews Peffer	
Sgt. George Perry	
Sgt. John Ruth	
Cpl. Frederick E. Server	
Cpl. Christian Allspach	
Cpl. Patrick Cigan	
Cpl. Kermit G. Nail	
Trumpt. Christian Leitz	
Trumpt. Wheeler H. Polk	
Blksm. Thomas Hinton	
Far. Richard Coam	At Ft. Ellis, for duty
Sad. Robert Somers	
Pvt. Fowler R. Applegate	
John F. Atkinson	
Patrick F. Brady	At Ft. Ellis, for duty
Charles Baker	At Ft. Ellis, for duty
Morris Babitsch	At Ft. Ellis, for duty
Herbert Bixby	
John J. Clarkins	At old Ft. Pease, E.D. w/QMD
Thomas K. Collins	
James A. Chamberlain	

Pvt. Francis Conner	At Ft. Ellis, for duty
John Dale	
Wiley D. Dean	
John Dugan	
Herbert O. Evans	At old Ft. Pease
William H. Fletcher	At Ft. Ellis, for duty
Jacob Forren	At Ft. Ellis, for duty
John Fitzgerald	
Benjamin F. Harper	At Ft. Ellis, for duty
Edward J. Hamilton	At old Ft. Pease
Morris H. Huth	
John Irving	
John Keegan	At old Ft. Pease
John Kinsler	At Ft. Sanders, for duty
Jackson Kennedy	At old Ft. Pease
Joseph Kroll	
Michael Kearney	
Frederick R. King	At Ft. Sanders, for duty
Walter Lookstedt	
Francis Long	
Charles Mallis	
Michael McCaffery	
Henry W. Merrick	At Ft. Ellis, for duty
Alfred Norman	At Ft. Ellis, for duty
William G. Osborn	
William H. Power	At old Ft. Pease
James Rotchford	
George C. Smith	At old Ft. Pease
Watson P. Stone	
John Tavlane	At old Ft. Pease
Gotleib Voltz	At Ft. Ellis, for duty
Charles Webber	At old Ft. Pease
Thomas White	
Henry Young	At old Ft. Pease

A part of Major Brisbin's battalion of the command accompanying Brig. Gen. Terry, Company G had two officers and thirty-four men. Second Lt. McClernand was serving on Col. Gibbon's staff, in the field. See pages 83-84 regarding Col. Gibbon's absence on the day of the battle.

SECOND CAVALRY
COMPANY H

Capt. Edward Ball	Cmdg. Co.
1st Lt. James G. McAdams	
1st Sgt. John R. Elkins	
Sgt. Asa T. Merrill	At Ft. Ellis, sick
Sgt. Clifford Pearson	
Sgt. John McCabe	At old Ft. Pease, sick
Sgt. Frank Whitney	
Sgt. Thomas Kelly	
Cpl. Francis Stewart	
Cpl. Charles Grillon	
Cpl. Andrew Kennedy	
Trumpt. Thomas Carney	At old Ft. Pease, sick
Blksm. Charles Murrey	
Far. Edward Wells	
Sad. James Beverly	
Pvt. James Adams	
William Benson	
John Brown	
Mathew F. Canning	E.D. as hospital attendant
John Carroll	
James Carroll	
Patrick Claffy	At Ft. Ellis, sick
John Clark	
Henry C. Coales	At Ft. Ellis, sick
Joseph H. Davis	
James R. Dipp	
Martin Dooley	At Ft. Ellis, for duty
Patrick Donegan	At Ft. Ellis, for duty
Thomas Duffy	

Pvt. Joel S. Flanigan
    Thomas B. Gilmore
    Henry E. Gray   At old Ft. Pease, sick
    Thomas S. Hoover
    Joseph Igglesden   At old Ft. Pease, E.D.
                         w/QMD
    Nicholas James   At old Ft. Pease, E.D.
                         w/Subs. Dept.

    George F. Kane
    Mathew Kearney   At Ft. Ellis, for duty
    John Kern
    Henry Kozigk   At Ft. Sanders, for duty
    George T. Lawlor
    Frederick Miller   At Ft. Ellis, for duty
    William Miller
    Thomas McDonald
    Victor McKelery
    George S. Meyers
    Daniel Mount   At Ft. Ellis, sick
    Francis Phillips
    Frank Ruland
    Henry Rahmeir   Killed by Indians, 23
                         May 1876

    John Reardon
    Henry Schargenstein
    Augustus Stocker   Killed by Indians, 23
                         May 1876

    Frank Walters
    Richard Walsh
    John B. Warren
    William Wherstedt
    William Wilson
    David H. Winters
    Edward Williams

A part of Major Brisbin's battalion of the command accompanying Brig. Gen. Terry, Company H had two officers and forty-one men. Second Lt. Lovell H. Jerome was in arrest at Fort Ellis since 17 Mar. 1876. Pvts. Rahmeir and Stocker were the two men who, along with citizen-teamster Quinn were attacked and killed while hunting away from the camp. See pages 83-84 regarding Col. Gibbon's absence on the day of the battle.

SECOND CAVALRY
COMPANY L

Capt. Lewis Thompson	Cmdg. Co.
1st Lt. Samuel T. Hamilton	
2nd Lt. Charles B. Schofield	Battalion Adjutant
1st Sgt. Henry Wilkins	
Sgt. Emil Plum	
Sgt. Charles E. Weston	
Sgt. Edward Page	
Sgt. John F. McBlain	
Sgt. John F. Prutting	
Cpl. Charles Egert	
Cpl. William Thompson	
Cpl. Martin Shannon	
Cpl. Robert A. McLeod	At Ft. Ellis, for duty
Trumpt. Harry B. Melville	
Trumpt. James H. White	
Blksm. Samuel A. Glass	
Far. Ansil Riden	
Sad. John Cox	
Pvt. Konrad Bubenheim	
John C. Chase	
Wilfred Clark	Confined Ft. Ellis 4 May 1876
George Cook	
John W. Davis	
Charles R. Davis	
Pierre Domminger	At Ft. Sanders, for duty
John Engleson	At Ft. Ellis, sick
John Flanigan	

Pvt. Samuel Foulks	At Ft. Ellis, sick
Daniel Gallagher	
Samuel Hendrickson	
Michael Hog	At Ft. Ellis, for duty
William H. Jones	
William Jenkins	
Michael Kelly	
Philip Low	At old Ft. Pease
Maurice Murphy	At Ft. Ellis, for duty
David Murphy	
Jean J. Malcolm	
Frank P. Miller	At Ft. Ellis, for duty
Jacob Mauren	
John O'Conner	
James Ryan	
Abram W. Riley	At Ft. Ellis, for duty
Maxim Robideau	
John Rockil	Confined Ft. Ellis
James Sanderson	
Charles Stevens	At old Ft. Pease, E.D. w/QMD
Robert Sturm	At old Ft. Pease
John Thompson	
George T. Waddington	At Ft. Ellis, for duty
Joseph Whalen	
John Winkle	
Arthur Ward	
Wade H. Young	

A part of Major Brisbin's battalion of the command accompanying Brig. Gen. Terry, Company L had three officers and thirty-seven men. See pages 83-84 regarding Col. Gibbon's absence on the day of the battle.

SIXTH INFANTRY
COMPANY C

Capt. James W. Powell	Cmdg. Co.
2nd Lt. Bernard A. Byrne	Bn. ACS & AAQM, Depot Commissary
1st Sgt. Edward B. Hanson	
Sgt. John Scott	On steamer "Josephine" for duty
Sgt. Michael Morris	
Sgt. James Dooley	
Sgt. Frederick Seaver	
Cpl. Charles Randolph	
Cpl. Charles Muessigbrodt	
Cpl. William S. Doyle	On steamer "Josephine" for duty
Cpl. George W. Crans	
Musc. Michael Foley	
Artif. Hans Storm	
Artif. Emanuel L. Hoffman	
Pvt. James Armstrong	At Ft. Buford, for duty
Robert D. Atcheson	
James Bisbing	
Joseph Broderick	
William H. Brown	
John H. Cassidy	On steamer "Josephine" for duty
William H. Cecil	
Warner Colwell	
Daniel Corcoran	
William W. Feaha	

Pvt. Edward Felber	On steamer "Josephine" for duty
William A. Hall	
Henry Hamilton	
Leslie Haven	E.D. as hospital steward since 14 May 1876
Joseph Jacobs	
John Kenny	
Jeremiah Kieley	Confined in the field 28 June 1876
Louis Kamer	On steamer "Josephine" for duty
Daniel Maloney	
Thomas Mathews	
Joseph McElevey	
George Monach	
Patrick Murphy	
Albert Phelps	On steamer "Josephine" for duty
August Reis	
William F. Sagle	
Charles Schwab	On steamer "Josephine" for duty
John J. Shaw	At Ft. Buford, for duty
Charles Simon	
Julius Simonson	On steamer "Josephine" for duty
Frederick W. Smith	
Henry J. Smith	
Henry C. Soltneidel	
George W. Stephens	Deserted 18 May 1876
Richard Thornton	
William H. Wiggins	

A part of Major Moore's battalion, Company C was at the Powder River Camp with two officers and thirty-seven men. First Lt. Eugene B. Gibbs was on Detached Service as Aide-de-Camp to Brig. Gen. Alfred H. Terry (has never joined the company).

SIXTH INFANTRY
COMPANY D

Capt. Daniel H. Murdock   Cmdg. Co.

1st Lt. Frederick W. Thibaut   Cmdg. escort on steamer
"Josephine"

1st Sgt. John J. Bowman

Sgt. Alexander Wyley   On steamer "Josephine"
for duty

Sgt. William G. Gayle

Sgt. Joseph Fox

Sgt. Henry Fox   Drowned while ferrying
mail 12 June 1876

Cpl. Samuel McLaughlin

Cpl. James P. Foreaker

Cpl. James W. Rodgers

Cpl. Charles F. Lawson

Trumpt. William Copestick

Drum. Garrison Redd   Discharged in the field
24 May 1876

Pvt. Elmore Bradley

   Jenson Campbell   At Ft. Buford, for duty

   Thomas Clark

   Michael Connell

   George Cook   Confined Newport, Ky.
27 Oct. 1875

   James Costigan   Confined in the field

   James Daly   On steamer "Josephine"
for duty

   Daniel Deegan

   Thomas Gibney   On steamer "Josephine"
for duty

Pvt. William Gibson	At Ft. Buford, sick
Ole Halverson	
Angelo Howard	
George Howard	
Henry Howard	
Frank Hughes	
Albert A. Hummell	
Alexander Kinman	At Ft. Buford, dischgd. 17 May 1876
John Maley	
Martin McGowan	
John W. Michley	
William J. Mulhern	On steamer "Josephine" for duty
William M. Palmer	On steamer "Josephine" for duty
Jacob Pippher	
Martin Ramey	
Webster Rednor	
David Robinson	
Wilmot P. Sanford	
Thomas R. Smiley	
Levi A. Stone	
Samuel E. Teeters	
Aaron T. Weierbach	
James Winn	

A part of Major Moore's battalion, Company D was at the Powder River Camp with one officer and thirty-two men. First Lt. Thibaut was commanding the escort aboard the steamer "Josephine" en route to Fort Buford, and 2nd Lt. Thomas G. Townsend was absent on leave since 1 Sept. 1875.

SIXTH INFANTRY
COMPANY I

2nd Lt. George B. Walker   Cmdg. Co.
1st Sgt. Oscar W. Litchfield
Sgt. George H. Love
Sgt. Dennis Donavan
Sgt. George Walker   Acting Sgt. Maj. of
                 battalion in the field

Sgt. Charles Roberts
Cpl. Samuel L. Middaugh
Cpl. Liemon P. Lyon   On leave 19 June 1876
Cpl. George McKee
Cpl. Charles H. Adams
Musc. Louis Wahler
Pvt. William S. Beaver
     Patrick Boyle
     Michael Buggle
     Peter F. Clarison
     John Craig
     John H. Drusselmeir
     John Dunlap   On steamer "Josephine"
                   for duty

     Thomas Enright
     Sylvester Fitzpatrick
     John F. Frank
     Henry Hammond   Deserted 20 June 1876
     Charles Johnson
     Griffith Jones
     Charles Kulp   At Ft. Buford, for duty
     John Leonard

Pvt. Amos W. Littlejohn	On steamer "Josephine" for duty
William Magee	
Hugh McLaughlin	
Anton Muller	Confined Stillwater, Minn.
Thomas Murphy	At Ft. Buford, died 23 May 1876
Peter O' Donnell	
James E. Redd	
Dennis Ring	
Thomas Sanders	
William A. Sartain	On steamer "Josephine" for duty
August Schomberg	
Benjamin F. Shortis	
Jacob Smith	
John Smith	
Charlie Stierle	
John J. Sttuka	On steamer "Josephine" for duty
Joseph Thalon	
John Walsh	
John C. Warner	Returned from leave 24 June 1876

A part of Major Moore's battalion, Company I was at the Powder River Camp with one officer and thirty-five men. Capt. Edward R. Ames was on leave since 29 Feb. 1876, and 1st Lt. Jacob F. Munson was on General Recruiting Duty since 11 Sept. 1874.

TWENTIETH INFANTRY
GATLING GUN DETACHMENT

2nd Lieut. William H. Low, Jr.	Co. C	
2nd Lieut. Frank X. Kinzie	Co. F	
Sgt. Hugh Hynds	Co. B	
Cpl. Jacob W. Crawford	Co. B	
Pvt. Patrick Collins	Co. B	sick at Fort Lincoln
Phillip W. Devereaux	Co. B	D.S. w/Co. B, 6th Inf.
Rufus Henderson	Co. B	
Sgt. Lafayette Davis	Co. C	
Pvt. Thomas F. Boen	Co. C	
William A. Ellis	Co. C	
John McCormick	Co. C	
Edward McDonald	Co. C	
Pvt. Edward Lowell	Co. D	
George Rivers	Co. D	
Cpl. Peter G. Burdeff	Co. F	
Pvt. Neal Devlin	Co. F	
James Gordon	Co. F	
Thomas Powers	Co. F	
William Robinson	Co. F	
William G. Smith	Co. F	
Cpl. Thomas Tully	Co. G	D.S. w/Co. B, 6th Inf.
Pvt. James J. McGirr	Co. G	D.S. w/Co. B, 6th Inf.
Cpl. Thomas F. Oldsworth	Co. H	
Pvt. James Gomely	Co. H	
Napoleon Miller	Co. H	

Pvt. John Pangburn	Co. H	
James Shields	Co. H	
Sgt. Peter E. Monaghan	Co. I	D.S. w/Co. B, 6th Inf.
Sgt. Edward Alexander	Co. I	
Pvt. Charles Birns	Co. I	D.S. w/Co. B, 6th Inf.
William Kelly	Co. I	
John Mains	Co. I	D.S. w/Co. B, 6th Inf.

SIXTH INFANTRY
COMPANY B

Capt. Stephen Baker	Cmdg. Co.
1st Lt. John Carland	
1st Sgt. Thomas Farrell	
Sgt. Solomon Savage	Dischgd. in the field 26 May 1876
Sgt. Hugh Kernan	
Sgt. Charlie Griswold	At Ft. Lincoln, for duty
Sgt. William Brinkman	
Cpl. William R. Mooney	
Cpl. Peter Engelhardt	
Musc. James Sharlett	
Musc. Daniel DeLany	
Pvt. James Armstrong	
Charles Birach	
Albert E. Brown	
William Buckley	
James Cameron	
James Clark	
William Costigan	
Patrick N. Crowley	
John Dark	
John Duffy	
Spencer Edwards	
John Falardo	
William Finnegan	At Powder River Camp
Patrick Fitzimmons	
Julius B. Fleming	
Isaac Hedden	At Ft. Lincoln, for duty
Robert F. Jones	

Pvt. Barney Kamphouse
 John Kistler
 William Langton
 James Martin
 Michael McCarthy
 Patrick F. McCarthy
 Michael G. Minchin
 James Murray
 Thomas Nolan
 John O'Conners
 Charles D. Palmer   At Powder River Camp
 James Reedy   At Ft. Lincoln, for duty
 John Sarratt
 William Scott
 Conrad Sieffert
 Edward T. Spring
 Thomas Whalen   Confined Fargo, D.T., 23
          June 1876
 George Withrow

Temporarily attached for duty at camp on Little Missouri 29 May 1876, from 20th Infantry, Companies as indicated:

 Sgt. Peter E. Monahan [*sic*] Co. D [? Co. I]
 Cpl. Thomas Tully   Co. G
 Pvt. Philip N. Devereaux Co. D [? Co. B]
  James McGirr   Co. G
  Charles Birns   Co. G [? Co. I]
  John Mavis [Mains] Co. G

A part of Brig. Gen. Terry's escort, Company B was on board the steamer "Far West" with two officers and forty-four men. Second Lt. Charles H. Ingalls was appointed on 29 Feb. 1876 and granted 30 days leave from 29 Mar. 1876 before reporting to Fort Columbus, N.Y.

SEVENTEENTH INFANTRY
COMPANY C

Capt. Malcolm McArthur	Cmdg. Co.
1st Lt. Frank D. Garretty	
2nd Lt. James D. Nickerson	
1st Sgt. James Johnston	At Ft. Wadsworth, sick
Sgt. Charles Smith	
Sgt. Daniel O'Grady	At Ft. Wadsworth, sick
Sgt. Eugene Snow	
Sgt. Joseph Marchand	
Cpl. Patrick Mulcahy	
Cpl. Anton Schindler	At Ft. Abercrombie, for duty 19 Oct. 1874
Cpl. James Dignon	
Cpl. Carl Kohlepp	
Pvt. Sanford F. Brown	
Charles Becker	
Frank F. Bang	
John Curtis	
John H. Cummins	
William H. Crosby	Confined in the field
Leonard Deitz	
Charles Fox	
Richard Fowler	
Joseph Greenwald	
James Gruver	
Thomas W. Graham	
William Harris	
Joseph Heuser	
John Hunter	
Boward Hussey	Deserted 17 May 1876

Pvt. Andrew Johnson   E.D. as hospital attendant
since 1 May 1876

Martin Kruger
James Kelly
Fred H. Little   At St. Paul, Minn., for
duty 5 Oct. 1875

Louis P. Milligan
James McElroy
William McLain
George McAlvey
William Miller   At Ft. Wadsworth, sick
Charles Odeu
John H. Perkins
Eli Prescott
John J. Phillips
Thomas Plunkett
Thomas W. Rance
Casper Strohm
Alex F. Smith
John Speirs
Robert Sproul
Frank Shepler
John E. Spalding
Charles H. Stewart
Hugh C. Thompson
Frank H. Thomas
John L. Waldo

A part of Brig. Gen. Terry's escort, Company C was
at the Powder River Camp with three officers and forty-
four men.

SEVENTEENTH INFANTRY
COMPANY G

Capt. Louis H. Sanger   Cmdg. Co.
1st Lt. Josiah Chance   Depot Quartermaster
2nd Lt. Henry P. Walker
1st Sgt. William Bolton
Sgt. George F. W. Miller
Sgt. William Mayer
Sgt. Frank E. Osgood
Sgt. James Hewitt
Cpl. John Stanley
Cpl. David Street
Cpl. John McCarthy
Cpl. Thomas Parnell
Musc. Michael Crowley
Artif. James Brierly
Pvt. Charles F. Almon
    Darian W. Batterall
    Charles Beckman
    Frederick G. Bond
    Herman Binkhoff
    William Butler
    John Casey
    Charles Carlton   At Ft. Lincoln, for duty
    Samuel Cling
    Albert Davis
    Owen P. Duffy
    Daniel Dixon   At Washington, D.C.,
                               Insane Asylum 14
                               Sept. 1874

Pvt. George Ferrers
　　Martin Gannon
　　William Hammond　　At Ft. Lincoln, sick
　　Henry Keeler
　　George Kellerman
　　Charles A. Kelly　　At Ft. Lincoln, sick
　　Max W. Kistner　　At Ft. Lincoln, for duty
　　John Lyons
　　John D. Massingale
　　Eben A. Maxfield　　At Ft. Lincoln, for duty
　　Francis Marriaggi
　　Charles Muller
　　John McCarthy
　　Edward B. McCarthy
　　Charles Miller (1st)
　　Charles Miller (2nd)
　　William Myers
　　Fulton A. Nichols
　　Louis R. Nieschang
　　Terence O'Brien
　　John Petit
　　William Ritchart
　　Thomas Rogers
　　Walter Seamon
　　Francis A. Steele
　　Philip Trotvine
　　Maurice Ward
　　John Whitford

A part of Brig. Gen. Terry's escort, Company G was at the Powder River Camp with three officers and forty-five men.

SEVENTH CAVALRY
HEADQUARTERS

Col. Samuel D. Sturgis	D.S. at St. Louis, Mo.
Lt. Col. George A. Custer	Cmdg. Regt., killed
Maj. Joseph G. Tilford	On leave
Maj. Lewis Merrill	D.S. at Philadelphia, Pa.
Maj. Marcus A. Reno	
Adjt. 1st Lt. William W. Cooke	Killed
RQM. 1st Lt. Henry J. Nowlan	D.S. as AAQM on Brig. Gen. Terry's staff
Vet. Surg. C. A. Stein	At Powder River Camp
Sgt. Maj. William H. Sharrow	Killed
QM Sgt. Thomas Causby	At Powder River Camp
Sad. Sgt. John G. Tritten	At Powder River Camp
Chf. Trumpt. Henry Voss	Killed

SEVENTH CAVALRY
BAND

Chf. Musc. Felix V. Vinatieri	At Powder River Camp
Pvt. Otto Arndt	At Powder River Camp
Conrad Baumbach	At Powder River Camp
Benjamin Beck	At Powder River Camp
Edmond Burlis	At Powder River Camp
Andrew Carter	At Powder River Camp
Joseph Carroll	At Powder River Camp
Peter Eisenberger	At Powder River Camp
Jacob Emerich	At Powder River Camp
Julius Griesner	At Powder River Camp
Julius Jungsbluth	At Powder River Camp
Joseph Kneublucher	At Ft. Lincoln, sick
Frank Lombard	At Ft. Lincoln, sick
George A. Merritt	At Ft. Lincoln, sick
Bernard O'Neill	At Powder River Camp
George Rudolph	At Powder River Camp
Thomas Sherbon	At Powder River Camp

SEVENTH CAVALRY
COMPANY A

Capt. Myles Moylan	Cmdg. Co.
1st Lt. Charles C. DeRudio	TDy from Co. E
2nd Lt. Charles A. Varnum	Cmdg. Indian Scouts
1st Sgt. William Heyn	Wounded
Sgt. Roland W. Corwine	At Ft. Lincoln, dischgd. 29 May 1876
Sgt. Henry Fehler	
Sgt. Samuel Alcott	At Powder River Camp
Sgt. George McDermott	
Sgt. Ferdinand A. Culbertson	
Cpl. John Thomas Easley	Promoted Sgt. 1 June 1876
Cpl. John F. Cody	At Ft. Lincoln, dischgd. 22 June 1876
Cpl. James Dalious	Killed
Cpl. Stanislaus Roy	
Trumpt. William G. Hardy	
Trumpt. David McVeigh	
Blksm. Andrew Hamilton	
Far. John Bringes	
Sad. John Muering	
Pvt. Charles Aller	
John E. Armstrong	Killed
August Bockerman	At Powder River Camp
Neil Bancroft	
Louis Baumgartner	
Benjamin F. Burdick	At Powder River Camp
Wilbur F. Blair	
Thomas Blake	

Pvt. George Bott
    Andrew Conner
    Cornelius Cowley
    Jacob Diehle   Wounded
    Michael Coveney   Deserted 17 May 1876
    James Drinan   Killed
    Otto Durselew
    Samuel Foster   Wounded
    John W. Franklin
    John M. Gilbert
    Edwin Grant   At Ft. Lincoln, dischgd.
                      8 May 1876

    David W. Harris
    Charles Heywood   At Ft. Lincoln, dischgd.
                      14 May 1876

    Frederick Holmstead   Wounded
    Stanton Hook
    Emil O. Ionson
    Samuel Johnson
    Denis Kerr   At Ft. Lincoln, for duty
    George H. King   Promoted Cpl. 1 June
                      1876, wounded

    William McClurg
    James McDonald   Killed
    William Moody   Killed
    William D. Nugent
    Rufus C. Pickering   At Ft. Lincoln, dischgd.
                      14 May 1876
    John Lamb   Deserted 15 May 1876
    George W. Procter
    John Ragsdale   At Powder River Camp
    Francis M. Reeves   Wounded
    Richard Rollins   Killed
    Thomas Seayers

155

Pvt. Anton Siebelder
    Elijah T. Strode   Wounded
    John Sullivan   Killed
    Thomas P. Sweetzer   Killed
    William O. Taylor
    Howard H. Weaver
    John Weis   At Ft. Lincoln, for duty

A part of Major Reno's battalion. Company A had two officers and forty-eight men participating in the Battle of the Little Big Horn. First Lt. A. E. Smith was on TDy commanding Company E and 2nd Lt. Varnum commanded the scouts.

SEVENTH CAVALRY
COMPANY B

Capt. Thomas M. McDougall — Cmdg. Co.

2nd Lt. Benjamin H. Hodgson — TDy as Bn. Adjt. to Major Reno; killed

1st Sgt. James Hill

Sgt. Peter Gannon — At Powder River Camp

Sgt. Rufus D. Hutchinson

Sgt. Daniel Carroll — At Ft. Lincoln, for duty

Sgt. Thomas Murray

Sgt. Benjamin C. Criswell — Promoted Sgt. 4 June 1876

Cpl. James Dougherty

Cpl. Charles Cunningham — Wounded

Cpl. William M. Smith — Promoted Cpl. 15 May 1876, wounded

Cpl. Adam Wetzel — Promoted Cpl. 4 June 1876

Trumpt. John Connell — At Powder River Camp

Trumpt. James Kelly

Blksm. John Crump — Appointed Blksm. 15 May 1876

Far. James E. Moore

Sad. John E. Bailey

Pvt. James A. Abos — Confined Ft. Richardson, Tex., 1 May 1876

Peter O. Barry

James F. Barsantee

William Boam

Hugh Bonner

Pvt. Ansgarius Boren
    George Brainard
    James Brown   At Powder River Camp
    Charles Burns   At Powder River Camp
    William M. Caldwell At Powder River Camp
    James Callan   At Powder River Camp
    Thomas J. Callan
    Charles A. Campbell Reduced from Sgt.
                        4 June 1876

    John J. Casey
    Thomas Carmody
    Harry Criswell
    Frank Clark
    Thomas W. Coleman
    Michael Crowe
    Patrick Crowley
    William H. Davenport
    Louis DeTourriel   At Powder River Camp
    Augustus L. DeVoto
    Jacob W. Doll   At Powder River Camp
    Richard Dorn   Killed
    William Frank
    Frederick H.
      Gehrmann   At Powder River Camp
    John Gray   At Powder River Camp
    John J. Keefe   At Powder River Camp
    Ferdinand Klaweitter At Powder River Camp
    David W. Lewis   Confined Ft. Barrancas,
                        Fla., 26 Apr. 1876

    John L. Littlefield   At Powder River Camp
    George B. Mack   Killed
    William Martin
    John McCabe

Pvt. Bernard McGurn   At Powder River Camp
    Terrence McLaughlin
    William McMasters
    William E. Morrow   At Powder River Camp
    Thomas O'Brien   At Powder River Camp
    James O'Neill   At Ft. Lincoln, sick
    John O'Neill
    James Pym
    George F. Randall
    Stephen L. Ryan
    Hiram W. Sager
    Daniel Shea
    Patrick Simons   At Powder River Camp
    Philip Spinner
    Edward Stout
    James Thomas
    Henry L. Tinkham   At Powder River Camp
    William Trumble
    Richard A. Wallace
    Edwin B. Wright   At Powder River Camp
    Aaron Woods

Escorting the pack-train in the rear of the command, Company B had one officer and forty-eight men participating in the Battle of the Little Big Horn. First Lt. William T. Craycroft was ordered to appear before the Retiring Board, 18 May 1876, and 2nd Lt. Hodgson was adjutant for Reno's battalion.

SEVENTH CAVALRY
COMPANY C

Capt. Thomas W. Custer	Cmdg. Co., killed
2nd Lt. Henry M. Harrington	Killed
1st Sgt. Edwin Bobo	Killed
Sgt. Jeremiah Finley	Killed
Sgt. August Finckle	Killed
Sgt. Edwin Miller	At Ft. Lincoln, for duty
Sgt. Daniel A. Kanipe	[courier to pack train]
Sgt. Richard P. Hanley	[with pack train]
Cpl. Charles A. Crandall	At Powder River Camp
Cpl. Henry E. French	Killed
Cpl. John Foley	Killed
Cpl. Daniel Ryan	Killed
Trumpt. Thomas J. Bucknell	Killed
Trumpt. William Kramer	Killed
Blksm. John Fitzgerald	At Powder River Camp
Far. John King	Killed
Sad. George Howell	Killed
Wag. Frank Starck	At Powder River Camp
Pvt. Fred C. Allan	Killed
Charles L. Anderson	Deserted June 1876
Herbert Arnold	At Ft. Lincoln, for duty
James C. Bennett	Wounded [with pack train]
Charles H. Bischoff	At Powder River Camp
William Brandal	At Powder River Camp
John Brennan	[straggler; horse gave out; joined Reno]
John Brightfield	Killed

Pvt. John Corcoran	Confined Ft. Lincoln 5 May 1876
Christopher Criddle	Killed
George Eiseman	Killed
Gustave Engle	Killed
James Farrand	Killed
Morris Farrer	[disposition unknown]
Isaac Fowler	[with pack train]
Patrick Griffen	Killed
James Hathersall	Killed
John Jordan	[with pack train]
William Kane	At Powder River Camp, sick
John Lewis	Killed
Meredith Lovett	At Ft. Lincoln, sick
John Mahoney	[disposition unknown]
Thomas McCreedy	At Ft. Lincoln, for duty
John McGuire	[with pack train; wounded]
August Meyer	Killed
Frederick Meier	Killed
Martin Mullin	[disposition unknown]
Ottocar Nitsche	[with pack train]
Charles M. Orr	At Powder River Camp
Edgar Phillips	Killed
John Rauter	Killed
Edward Rix	Killed
James H. Russell	Killed
Ludwick St. John	Killed
Samuel S. Shade	Killed
Jeremiah Shea	Killed
Nathan Short	Killed
Alpheus Stuart	Killed
Ignatz Stungwitz	Killed

Pvt. Charles A. Steck	At Ft. Lincoln, dishon. dischgd. 10 May 1876
John Thadus	Killed
Peter Thompson	Wounded [straggler; horse gave out; joined Reno]
Garret Van Allen	Killed
Jacob Vahlert	At Ft. Lincoln, sick
Julius Van Arnim	At Powder River Camp
Robert Walker	At Powder River Camp
Oscar L. Warner	Killed
James Watson	[straggler; horse gave out; joined Reno]
Alfred Whittaker	Wounded [with pack train]
Willis B. Wright	Killed
Henry Wyman	Killed

A part of the battalion under Lt. Col. Custer's personal command, Company C had two officers and fifty men participating in the Battle of the Little Big Horn. First Lt. James Calhoun was on temporary duty commanding Company L.   Information in [brackets] is not on the official muster rolls, but reflects the personal research of the late Robert B. MacLaine.

SEVENTH CAVALRY
COMPANY D

Capt. Thomas B. Weir	Cmdg. Co.
2nd Lt. Winfield S. Edgerly	
1st Sgt. Michael Martin	
Sgt. Thomas Morton	At Ft. Lincoln, sick
Sgt. Thomas W. Harrison	
Sgt. James Flanagan	
Sgt. Thomas Russell	Promoted Sgt. 6 June 1876
Cpl. Albert Cunningham	At Powder River Camp
Cpl. George W. Wylie	
Trumpt. Aloys Bohner	
Trumpt. James McElroy	At Ft. Lincoln, dischgd. 8 May 1876
Blksm. Frederick Deitline	
Far. Vincent Charley	Killed
Sad. John Myers	
Pvt. James H. Alberts	
John B. Ascough	
Abraham B. Brant	
Thomas Conlan	
Thomas Cox	
Stephen Cowley	At Powder River Camp
George Dann	
David E. Dawsey	
Clarence F. Day	At Ft. Lincoln, dischgd. 19 May 1876
John J. Fay	
Harry A. Fox	At Powder River Camp
John Fox	

Pvt. Patrick M. Golden	Killed
Joseph Green	
John Green	At Powder River Camp
Gustav Harlinger	At Powder River Camp
Edward Hall	At Ft. Lincoln, for duty
Curtis Hall	
William Hardden	
James Harris	
William M. Harris	
John Hayer	
Jacob Hetler	Wounded
Henry Holden	
George Horn	
Charles H. Houghtaling	
Edward Housen	Killed
George Hunt	
James Hurd	
James Kavanagh	
John Keller	
Fremont Kipp	
John Kretchmer	
Jesse Kuehl	At Powder River Camp
Uriah S. Lewis	At Powder River Camp
William Muelling	At Ft. Lincoln, for duty
David Manning	
William A. Marshall	
John Meadwell	
Patrick McDonnel	
William O'Mann	
John Quinn	At Powder River Camp
William J. Randall	
Elwyn S. Reid	
William Sadler	
Charles Sanders	

Pvt. George Scott
   Henry G. Smith
   William E. Smith
   Thomas W. Stivers
   Frank Tolan
   Charles H. Welch
   James Wynn

A part of Capt. Benteen's battalion, Company D had two officers and fifty-two men participating in the Battle of the Little Big Horn. First Lt. James M. Bell was on six months leave since 24 Mar. 1876.

SEVENTH CAVALRY
COMPANY E

1st Lt. Algernon E. Smith	TDy from Co. A, Cmdg. Co., killed
2nd Lt. James G. Sturgis	TDy from Co. M, killed
1st Sgt. Frederick Hohmeyer	Killed
Sgt. John S. Wells	Relieved as 1st Sgt. 1 May 1876, on leave
Sgt. John S. Ogden	Killed
Sgt. William B. James	Killed
Sgt. James T. Riley	Wounded [with pack train]
Sgt. Lawrence Murphy	At Powder River Camp ?
Cpl. Thomas Hagan	Killed
Cpl. Henry S. Mason	Killed
Cpl. George C. Brown	Killed
Cpl. Albert H. Meyer	Killed
Trumpt. Thomas McElroy	Killed
Trumpt. George A. Moonie	Killed
Blksm. Henry Miller	At Powder River Camp ?
Far. Abel B. Spencer	At Powder River Camp ?
Sad. William Shields	At Powder River Camp ?
Pvt. Harry Abbots	E.D. as hospital attendant since 17 May 1876 [with Reno]
David Ackinson	On steamer "Far West," sick
William H. Baker	Killed
Robert Barth	Killed
Frank Berwald	At Powder River Camp ?
Owen Boyle	Killed

166

Pvt. James Brogan	Killed
Latrobe Bromwell	[with pack train]
August Brumm	At Ft. Lincoln, for duty
William H. Chapman	At Powder River Camp ?
Edward Conner	Killed
John Darris	Killed
William Davis	Killed
Richard Farrell	Killed
Julius Gilbert	At Ft. Lincoln, for duty
John Heim	Killed
John Henderson	Killed
Sykes Henderson	Killed
William Hieber	Killed
John Hiley	Killed
Frank Howard	At Ft. Lincoln, for duty
Anton Hutter	At Washington, D.C., Insane Asylum 9 June 1872
John James	[with pack train]
John G. Kimm	[with pack train]
Andy Knecht	Killed
Henry Lang	[with pack train]
Herod T. Liddiard	Killed
Patrick McCann	Confined Ft. Lincoln 17 May 1876
John McKenna	[with pack train]
Patrick O'Conner	Killed
Francis O'Toole	[with pack train]
Christopher Pandtle	E.D. as hospital attendant since 17 May 1876 [with Reno]
William Reese	At Powder River Camp ?
William H. Rees	Killed
Edward Rood	Killed

Pvt. Henry Schele	Killed
William Smallwood	Killed
Albert A. Smith	Killed
James Smith [1st]	Killed
James Smith [2nd]	Killed
Benjamin Stafford	Killed
Alexander Stella	Killed
William A. Torrey	Killed
Cornelius Van Sant	Killed
George Walker	Killed
Jerry Woodruff	At Ft. Lincoln, for duty

A part of the battalion under Lt. Col. Custer's personal command, Company E had two officers and forty-six men participating in the Battle of the Little Big Horn. Capt. Charles S. Ilsley was on Detached Service as Aide-de-Camp to Brig. Gen. John Pope since 30 Jan. 1868. First Lt. DeRudio was on temporary duty with Company A, and 2nd Lt. William VanW. Reily was on temporary duty with Company F. The muster-roll for this company does not indicate anyone as being at the supply depot on Powder River but does not give any other explanation for the seven men indicated by "?". Information in [brackets] is not on the official muster rolls, but reflects the personal research of the late Robert B. MacLaine.

SEVENTH CAVALRY
COMPANY F

Capt. George W. Yates	Cmdg. Co., killed
2nd Lt. William VanW. Reily	TDy from Co. E, killed
1st Sgt. Michael Kenny	Killed
Sgt. Frederick Nursey	Killed
Sgt. John Vickory	Killed
Sgt. John R. Wilkinson	Killed
Sgt. William Curtis	[with pack train]
Sgt. Henry Drago	At Ft. Lincoln, for duty
Cpl. Charles Coleman	Killed
Cpl. William Teeman	Killed
Cpl. John Briody	Killed
Cpl. Edward Clyde	At Powder River Camp ?
Blksm. James R. Manning	Killed
Far. Benjamin Brandon	Killed
Sad. Claus Schleiper	[with pack train]
Pvt. Thomas Atchison	Killed
William Brady	Killed
Benjamin F. Brown	Killed
Hiram E. Brown	At Powder River Camp ?
William Brown	Killed
Patrick Bruce	Killed
Lucien Burnham	Killed
James W. Butler	E.D. as hospital attendant since 17 May 1876 [with Reno]
James Carney	Killed
Armantheus D. Cather	Killed
Edward Davern	[orderly for Reno]

Pvt. Alexander Dowing	At Ft. Lincoln, for duty
Anton Dohman	Killed
Timothy Donnelly	Killed
William Eades	At Powder River Camp ?
Thomas J. Finnegan	[with pack train]
William Gardiner	Killed
William J. Gregg	At Powder River Camp ?
George W. Hammon	Killed
Leonard Harris	Confined Newport, Ky., 28 May 1875
Francis Hegner	At Powder River Camp ?
Frank Howard	[with pack train]
Frank Hunter	[with pack train]
Gustave Klein	Killed
Nikolaus Klein	At Ft. Lincoln, for duty
John Kelly	Killed
Herman Knauth	Killed
Meig Lefler	At Powder River Camp ?
William H. Lerock	Killed
Werner L. Lieman	Killed
William A. Lossee	Killed
Dennis Lynch	[with pack train]
Bernard Lyons	[with pack train]
Christian Madsen	Killed
Francis E. Milton	Killed
Joseph Milton	At Powder River Camp ?
Joseph Monroe	Killed
Frank Myers	At Powder River Camp ?
Ernest Meinike	At Ft. Lincoln, for duty
Sebastian Omling	Killed
Albert Pilcher	[with pack train]
Edwin H. Pickard	[sent to pack train]
James M. Rooney	[with pack train]
Michael Riley	At Powder River Camp ?

Pvt. Patrick Rudden	Killed
Richard Saunders	Killed
Frederick Shutte	[with pack train]
Francis W. Siefous	Killed
John W. Sweeney	[with pack train]
William Sweeney	Confined Bismarck, D.T., 23 Jan. 1876
George A. Warren	Killed
Michael Thorp	At Ft. Lincoln, for duty
Thomas Walsh	[with pack train]
Thomas N. Way	Killed
Paul Schleiforth	At Powder River Camp ?

A part of the battalion under Lt. Col. Custer's personal command, Company F had two officers and fifty-one men participating in the Battle of the Little Big Horn. First Lt. Henry Jackson was on Detached Service in Washington, D.C., since 9 Aug. 1871 (had not served with the Company since 28 Feb. 1868) and 2nd Lt. Charles W. Larned was on Detached Service at West Point N.Y., since 18 July 1874 (had not served with the Company since 4 Aug. 1873). The muster-roll for this company does not indicate anyone as being at the supply depot on Powder River but does not give any other explanation for the ten men indicated by "?". Information in [brackets] is not on the official muster rolls, but reflects the personal research of the late Robert B. MacLaine.

SEVENTH CAVALRY
COMPANY G

1st Lt. Donald McIntosh	Cmdg. Co., killed
2nd Lt. George D. Wallace	
1st Sgt. Edward Garlick	On leave since 30 Mar. 1876
Sgt. Edward Botzer	Killed
Sgt. Alexander Brown	
Sgt. Orlans Northeg	
Sgt. Martin Considine	Killed
Sgt. Frank Lloyd	At Ft. Lincoln, for duty
Cpl. James Martin	Killed
Cpl. Otto Hageman	Killed
Cpl. John E. Hammon	Promoted Sgt. 25 June 1876
Cpl. James Akers	Promoted Sgt. 25 June 1876
Trumpt. Henry Dose	Killed
Trumpt. Cassius R. Carter	At Shreveport, La., for duty since 19 Apr. 1876
Blksm. Walter O. Taylor	
Far. Benjamin Wells	Killed
Sad. Crawford Selby	Killed
Pvt. Charles Barney	At Powder River Camp
James P. Boyle	Wounded
Henry Brinkerhoff	Promoted Cpl. 25 June 1876
Melancthon H. Cressey	At Powder River Camp; Prom. Cpl. 25 June 1876

Pvt. Charles Campbell	Wounded
Edmond Dwyer	
Philip Flood	At Washington, D.C., Insane Asylum 1 May 1875
Theodore W. Goldin	
Thomas Graham	
William S. Gray	At Powder River Camp
Edward Grayson	
Frank G. Geist	At Powder River Camp
John Hackett	
George K. Henderson	At Powder River Camp
Benjamin Johnson	
Martin Kilfoyle	At Powder River Camp
Jacob Katzenmaier	At Powder River Camp
James Lawler	At Ft. Lincoln, for duty
Joseph Laden	At Ft. Lincoln, for duty
John Lattman	
Frank Lauper	At Powder River Camp
George Loyd	Promoted Cpl. 25 June 1876
Samuel McCormick	
John McDonnell	
John McEagan	
Hugh McGonigle	
John J. McGinniss	Killed
Edward D. McKay	At Powder River Camp
John McKee	At Powder River Camp
John McVay	Wounded
Andrew J. Moore	Killed
John Morrison	Wounded
Thomas O'Neill	
Henry Petring	

Pvt. John Rapp   Killed
  John A. Reed
  Eldorado I. Robb
  Robert Rowland   At Powder River Camp
  Benjamin F. Rogers Killed
  John R. Small
  Henry Seafferman At Powder River Camp
  John Shanahan   Killed
  Edward Stanley   Killed
  George W. Stephens At Powder River Camp
  Thomas Stevenson
  Daniel Sullivan   At Powder River Camp
  Joseph Tulo   At Powder River Camp
  Markus Weiss
  John W. Wallace   Promoted Cpl. 25 June
           1876
  Pasavan Williamson At Powder River Camp

A part of Major Reno's battalion, Company G had two officers and forty-three men participating in the Battle of the Little Big Horn. Capt. John E. Tourtelotte was on Detached Service as Col. & Aide-de-Camp to Gen. William T. Sherman since 31 Dec. 1870.

SEVENTH CAVALRY
COMPANY H

Capt. Frederick W. Benteen	Cmdg. Co.
1st Lt. Francis M. Gibson	
1st Sgt. Joseph McCurry	Wounded
Sgt. Patrick Conelly	Wounded
Sgt. John Pahl	Wounded
Sgt. Thomas McLaughlin	Wounded
Sgt. Mathew Moroney	
Sgt. George Geiger	
Cpl. George Lell	Killed
Cpl. Daniel Nealon	
Cpl. Alexander B. Bishop	Wounded
Trumpt. John Martin	
Trumpt. William Ramell	Wounded
Blksm. Henry W. B. Mechlin	
Far. John M. Marshall	At Ft. Rice, sick
Sad. Otto Voit	Wounded
Pvt. Jacob Adams	
Charles E. Avery	Confined Ft. Lincoln 17 May 1876
Henry Bishley	
Charles H. Bishop	Wounded
Henry Black	Wounded
James Boggs	At Ft. Rice, dischgd. 15 May 1876
William Channell	
John Cooper	Wounded
John Day	
George W. Dewey	
Edward Diamond	

Pvt. William Farley	Wounded
William George	Wounded
George W. Glease	
Timothy Haley	
Henry Haack	
Thomas Hughes	Wounded
Charles W. Hood	At Ft. Lincoln, sick
John Hunt	
George Kelly	
James Kelly	
Julien D. Jones	Killed
Frank Lambertin	At Ft. Lincoln, sick
Thomas Lawhorn	
Jan Maller	Wounded
John Muller	Confined Columbus Bks., Ohio, 22 Dec. 1875
Thomas McDermott	
James McNamara	
David McWilliams	At Powder River Camp, sick
Thomas Meador	Killed
Edler Nees	
Joshua S. Nicholas	
William O'Ryan	
John Phillips	Wounded
Francis Pitter	At Ft. Rice, sick
John S. Pinkston	
Samuel Severs	Wounded
David Taply	At Ft. Rice, sick
William C. Williams	
Aloyse L. Walter	At Powder River Camp
Charles Windolph	Wounded
Michael J. Walsh	Confined Jackson Bks., La., 10 May 1876

A part of Capt. Benteen's battalion, Company H had two officers and forty-five men participating in the Battle of the Little Big Horn. Second Lt. Ernest A. Garlington graduated from the Military Academy on 15 June 1876 and was assigned to the Company vice Lt. DeRudio promoted to Company E.

SEVENTH CAVALRY
COMPANY I

Capt. Myles W. Keogh	Cmdg. Co., killed
1st Lt. James E. Porter	Killed
1st Sgt. Frank E. Varden	Killed
Sgt. James Bustard	Killed
Sgt. Milton J. DeLacy	[with pack train]
Sgt. George Gaffney	With AAQM in the field, for duty
Sgt. Robert L. Murphy	With Dept. HQ in the field, for duty
Sgt. Michael Caddle	At Powder River Camp
Cpl. John Wild	Killed
Cpl. George C. Morriss	Killed
Cpl. Samuel F. Staples	Killed
Cpl. Joseph McCall	At Ft. Lincoln, for duty
Trumpt. John McGucker	Killed
Trumpt. John W. Patton	Killed
Blksm. Henry A. Bailey	Killed
Far. John Rivers	At Powder River Camp
Sad. George Haywood	At Ft. Lincoln, sick
Pvt. John Barry	Killed
Joseph H. Broadhurst	Killed
Franz C. Brown	With Maj. Reno, as clerk
David Cooney	Wounded [with pack train]
Thomas Conners	Killed
Thomas P. Downing	Killed
Edward Driscoll	Killed
Frederick Fox	At Ft. Lincoln, for duty
Conrad Faber	At St. Paul, Minn., for duty 2 Oct. 1874

178

Pvt. Gabriel Geesbacher	At Powder River Camp
Andrew Grimes	At Ft. Lincoln, for duty
David C. Gillette	Killed
George H. Gross	Killed
Adam Hetsimer	Killed
Edward P. Holcomb	Killed
Marion E. Horn	Killed
Charles L. Haack	At Ft. Lincoln, sick
Henry P. Jones	[with pack train]
Francis Johnson	[with pack train]
Gustave Korn	[straggler; horse gave out; joined Reno]
Patrick Kelly	Killed
Frederick Lehman	Killed
Henry Lehman	Killed
Edward W. Lloyd	Killed
Patrick Lynch	With Dept. HQ in the field, for duty
Mark E. Lee	On steamer "Far West," sick
Archibald McIlhargey	Killed
John McGinnis	At Ft. Lincoln, sick
James P. McNally	[with pack train]
John McShane	[with pack train]
John Mitchell	Killed
William E. Miller	At Ft. Lincoln, sick
Fred Myers	At Powder River Camp
Jacob Noshang	Killed
John O'Bryan	Killed
N. G. Owens	[with pack train]
George Post	Killed
John Parker	Killed
Felix James Pitter	Killed
John Porter	Confined Columbus Bks., Ohio, 1 June 1876

Pvt. James Quinn	Killed
Charles Ramsey	[with pack train]
William Reed	Killed
John W. Rossbury	Killed
Darwin L. Symms	Killed
Herbert P. Thomas	At Ft. Lincoln, for duty
James E. Troy	Killed
Charles Von Bramer	Killed
William B. Whaley	Killed
William Saas	At Ft. Lincoln, for duty

A part of the battalion under Lt. Col. Custer's personal command, Company I had two officers and forty-six men participating in the Battle of the Little Big Horn. Second Lt. Andrew H. Nave was absent on Sick Leave since 14 July 1874. Information in [brackets] is not on the official muster rolls, but reflects the personal research of the late Robert B. MacLaine.

SEVENTH CAVALRY
COMPANY K

1st Lt. Edward S. Godfrey	Cmdg. Co.
2nd Lt. Luther R. Hare	With Indian Scouts
1st Sgt. DeWitt Winney	Killed
Sgt. Robert M. Hughes	Killed
Sgt. Louis Rott	
Sgt. Andrew Frederick	
Sgt. Jeremiah Campbell	
Sgt. John Rafter	
Cpl. John Nolan	At Powder River Camp
Cpl. Henry Murray	At Powder River Camp
Cpl. John J. Callahan	Killed
Cpl. George Hose	Promoted Sgt. 12 July 1876
Trumpt. George B. Penwell	
Trumpt. Christian Schlafer	
Blksm. Edmund H. Burke	
Far. John R. Steintker	
Sad. Christian Boissen	
Wag. Albert Whytenfield	At Powder River Camp
Pvt. George Anderson	At Ft. Lincoln, for duty
Charles Ackerman	At Powder River Camp
Jacob Bauer	At Ft. Lincoln, sick
James Blair	At Ft. Lincoln, for duty
George Blunt	
Cornelius Bresnahan	
Joseph Brown	
Charles Burgdorf	At Powder River Camp
Charles Burkhardt	
Charles Chesterwood	

Pvt. Elihu F. Clear	Killed
Patrick Coakley	
William L. Crawford	At Powder River Camp
Patrick Corcoran	Wounded
Patrick Dooley	At Ft. Lincoln, sick
John Donohue	
Michael Delaney	
John Foley	
Charles Fisher	At Powder River Camp
William Gibbs	At McComb City, Miss., for duty
Julius Gunther	At Ft. Lincoln, sick
Thomas A. Gordon	
Thomas Green	At Powder River Camp
Julius Helmer	Killed
Andrew Holahan	At Powder River Camp
Walter Hoyt	At Powder River Camp
Jacob Horner	At Powder River Camp
Peter Jacobs	At McComb City, Miss., dischgd. 18 Apr. 1876
Alonzo Jennys	
William W. Lasley	
Andrew Lieberman	At Ft. Lincoln, for duty
Daniel Lyons	At Powder River Camp
Wilson McConnell	
Martin McCue	
Michael P. Madden	Wounded; promoted Sgt. 12 July 1876
Max Mielke	Wounded
Michael Murphy	
Thomas Murphy	
Michael Ragan	At Powder River Camp
Michael Reilly	At Powder River Camp
Francis Roth	At Powder River Camp

Pvt. Henry W. Rachel
    Jonathan Robers
    John Shauer
    John Schwerer
    August Siefert
    Frederick Smith   At Powder River Camp
    Emil Taube   At Powder River Camp
    William A. Van Pelt   At Powder River Camp
    Ernest Wasmus
    George A. Wilson   At Powder River Camp
    William Whitlow
    Henry Witt   At Powder River Camp

A part of Capt. Benteen's battalion, Company K had one officer and forty-one men participating in the Battle of the Little Big Horn. Capt. Owen Hale was on General Recruiting Duty at St. Louis, Mo., since 11 Sept. 1874, and 2nd Lt. Hare served with the scout detachment.

SEVENTH CAVALRY
COMPANY L

1st Lt. James Calhoun	TDy from Co. C, Cmdg. Co., killed
2nd Lt. John J. Crittenden	TDy from Co. G, 20th Inf., killed
1st Sgt. James Butler	Killed
Sgt. Henry Bender	At Powder River Camp
Sgt. William Cashan	Killed
Sgt. Amos B. Warren	Killed
Sgt. Hugo Finderson	At Ft. Lincoln, for duty
Sgt. John Mullan	[with pack train]
Cpl. William H. Harrison	Killed
Cpl. John Seiler	Killed
Cpl. John Minden	At Powder River Camp
Cpl. William H. Gilbert	Killed
Trumpt. Frederick Walsh	Killed
Blksm. Charles Siemon	Killed
Far. William H. Heath	Killed
Sad. Charles Perkins	Killed
Pvt. William G. Abrams	[with pack train]
George E. Adams	Killed
William Andrews	Killed
Anthony Assadely	Killed
Elmer Babcock	Killed
Charles Banks	[with pack train]
Nathan J. Brown	[disposition unknown]
John Burke	Killed
John Burkman	[with pack train]
Ami Cheever	Killed
Michael Conlan	At Ft. Lincoln, for duty

Pvt.	John R. Colwell	At Ft. Lincoln, sick
	William B. Crisfield	Killed
	William Dye	Killed
	John Duggan	Killed
	William Etzler	[with pack train]
	James J. Galvan	Killed
	Charles Graham	Killed
	Henry Hamilton	Killed
	Weston Harrington	Killed
	Louis Haugge	Killed
	Max Hoehn	At Powder River Camp
	Francis T. Hughes	Killed
	Thomas G. Kavanagh	Killed
	Michael Keegan	At Powder River Camp
	Ferdinand Leppler	At Powder River Camp, sick
	Louis Lobering	Killed
	William Logue	[disposition unknown]
	Charles McCarthy	Killed
	Peter McGue	Killed
	Bartholomew Mahoney	Killed
	Jasper Marshall	Wounded
	Philip McHugh	[with pack train]
	Alexander McPeak	At Powder River Camp
	Thomas E. Maxwell	Killed
	John Miller	Killed
	Lansing A. Moore	[disposition unknown]
	David J. O'Connell	Killed
	Christian Reibold	Killed
	Henry Roberts	Killed
	Walter B. Rogers	Killed
	Peter E. Rose	[with pack train]
	Charles Schmidt	Killed
	Charles Scott	Killed

Pvt. Bent Siemonson   Killed
    Andrew Snow   Killed
    Otto Sprague   At Ft. Lincoln, for duty
    Henry Stoffel   [with pack train]
    Timothy Sullivan   [with pack train]
    Byron Tarbox   Killed
    Edward D. Tessier   Killed
    Thomas S. Tweed   Killed
    Michael Vetter   Killed

A part of the battalion under Lt. Col. Custer's personal command, Company L had two officers and fifty-seven men participating in the Battle of the Little Big Horn. Capt. Michael V. Sheridan was on Detached Service as Aide-de-Camp to Lt. Gen. Philip H. Sheridan since 18 Feb. 1871, 1st Lt. Charles Braden was absent on Sick Leave since 5 Oct. 1875, and 2nd Lt. Edwin P. Eckerson was appointed on 2 May 1876, vice Lt. Braden promoted, and had not yet joined. Information in [brackets] is not on the official muster rolls, but reflects the personal research of the late Robert B. MacLaine.

SEVENTH CAVALRY
COMPANY M

Capt. Thomas H. French	Cmdg. Co.
1st Lt. Edward G. Mathey	Cmdg. the pack-train
1st Sgt. John M. Ryan	
Sgt. William Capes	At Powder River Camp
Sgt. Miles F. O'Hara	Killed
Sgt. Charles White	Wounded
Sgt. Patrick Carey	Wounded
Sgt. John McGlone	Promoted Sgt. 17 June 1876
Cpl. Henry M. Scollin	Killed
Cpl. Frederick Streing	Killed
Cpl. William Lalor	Promoted Cpl. 17 June 1876
Trumpt. Charles Fisher	
Trumpt. Henry C. Weaver	
Far. William M. Wood	At Ft. Rice, for duty
Sad. John Donohue	
Wag. Joseph Ricketts	At Powder River Camp
Pvt. John Bates	
Frank Bower	Confined Ft. Wayne, Mich., 10 Feb. 1876
Frank Braun	Wounded
Morris Cain	
Harris Davis	
John Dolan	Reduced from Sgt. 14 June 1876
Jean B. D. Gallenne	
Bernard Golden	
George Heid	

Pvt. Charles Kavannagh
    Henry Gordon   Killed
    Henry Klotzbucher   Killed
    George Lorentz   Killed
    James McCormick   At Powder River Camp
    Daniel Mahoney
    John H. Meier   Wounded
    Hugh N. Moore
    William D. Meyer   Killed
    William E. Morris   Wounded
    Daniel Newell   Wounded
    Frank Neely
    Edward Pigford
    William Robinson
    Roman Rutten   Wounded
    Hobart Ryder
    William W. Rye
    John Seamans
    Robert Senn
    James Severs
    John Sivertson
    William Slaper
    George E. Smith   Killed
    Frank Sniffen
    Walter S. Sterland   At Powder River Camp
    Frank Stratton
    David Summers   Killed
    James J. Tanner   Killed
    Levi Thornberry
    Rollins L. Thorpe
    Henry Turley   Killed
    Henry C. Voight   Killed
    Thomas B. Varner
    George Weaver

Pvt. James Weeks
 Charles G. Wiedman Wounded
 John Whisten
 James Wilbur   Wounded
 Charles Williams
 Ferdinand Widmayer At Powder River Camp
 John Zametzer

A part of Major Reno's battalion, Company M had one officer and fifty-seven men participating in the Battle of the Little Big Horn. First Lt. Mathey was commanding the pack-train and 2nd Lt. Sturgis was on temporary duty with Company E.

Index